THE GOD PROJECT

IF HE'S REAL,
HOW CAN HE BE REAL TO YOU?

SCOTT ZIEGLER

Choice Publishing
Des Plaines, Illinois

Ordering Information:
Quantity sales. Special discounts are available on quantity purchases by churches, ministries, and others. For details, contact the author at the email address above.

The God Project/ Scott Ziegler. —1st ed.
ISBN-13: 978-1981404384
ISBN-10: 1981404384

Contents

With appreciation to the people of The Bridge Community Church and Hillcrest Bible Church, who eagerly apply these teachings and demonstrate God's presence in every-day life.

Now set your mind and heart to seek the Lord your God.

—1 Chronicles 22:19

Introduction

I'm really glad you're interested in doing this study.

After all, this is more than a book to read. It's a project to undertake. But the result will be worth it. If there is a real God, it's hard to imagine anything more important for us to embark on, that will matter more in the long run, than knowing and relating to him.

That's what this project is all about.

There's a broad range of people who read this book and do the study. Some have no idea who God is, and are even wondering if he exists. If that's you, you are probably at least curious about what the Bible says about him...and what it says about you, or you wouldn't be reading this.

For others of you, you are sure God is real. Maybe because you grew up going to church, or you had parents who taught you about God, or you look around and see that there's no way this world could even exist if it wasn't for some kind of creator. So, you believe in him. But you don't know much about him, or what he wants *of* you and *for* you. And you want to know.

Some of you are going to church and maybe you've even taken that first critical step of faith. But you know you've got a lot to learn and a lot of growing to do.

So, you are reading this book and doing this study. Cool.

Here's how this works. This isn't really just a book. It's more than that. And it's not just a Bible study. It's kind of both, with possibly a bit of mentoring thrown in.

You probably got this book through a friend who offered to go through it with you, or from a church, where you were also assigned a study partner. Their part is to walk you through the study, helping you with questions, and talking with you about what you are reading and the Bible passages you'll be looking up. You'll probably find that those discussions will become catalysts for learning the material and the friendship you'll gain from meeting will last long after the study is complete.

If you are reading this book that way, with a study partner, then read it one chapter at a time and answer the questions in each section. There are several sections in each chapter. Once every week or two, you and your study partner will get together to review and discuss the questions you will have filled out.

If you picked this book up on your own, or someone gave it to you, welcome! You can still do this on your own. Just make sure you answer the questions as you read through the chapters. If you have additional questions or you need assistance understanding some things in the book, there's additional help available. I'm a pastor in a church with several other pastors and we'd be happy to respond to questions you might have. Just shoot us an email from this web page: thebridge.church/contact-us. One of our pastors will respond.

I think you'll find this to be one of the most valuable things you've ever been through, if you apply yourself and are committed to making your way through all the material with a mind to learn and a heart to grow. If you approach it this way, you'll do both, learn and grow. When it comes to a relationship with our creator, learning and growing is hugely valuable in and of itself. So, make the most of this and apply yourself.

About the Bible part. I'll explain in the first chapter why we are using the Bible for this study. But in the meantime, I get it that you might not be familiar with what is in it and how it is put together, and perhaps you're brand new to looking up passages in the Bible. You might have no idea how to find specific verses in the Bible. No problem.

If you are working with a study partner, the first time you get together (that might have been already), they will probably give you a Bible and show you how to find Bible verses in it.

But if you are doing this on your own, it's not hard. Use the Table of Contents at the front to find the book you are looking up, and then just look for the chapter and the verse. You can do it. I'll summarize it here, but you are probably familiar with it to some degree.

When a Bible verse is cited, the first thing you see is the name of the book. That's because the Bible itself is not really "a" book, but a collection of books, sixty-six of them. After the book name comes the chapter, and then the verse. Each book in the Bible is organized that way, with multiple chapters, and verses within those chapters.

Let me give you an example. Genesis 1:1 tells you to go to the very first verse in the Bible. Genesis is the first book (you can see that in the Table of Contents). Then you see 1:1, meaning chapter 1, verse 1. On the other end, Revelation 22:21 is the last verse in the Bible, because Revelation is the last book, chapter 22 is the last chapter in Revelation, and verse 21 is the last verse in chapter 22. Then there are all the verses in between. You find them the same way. Find the book, go to the chapter, and then the verse. See? Not hard at all.

It shouldn't take you more than an hour or two per chapter in this book. Then, about every two weeks, you will meet with your study partner and discuss the questions in the chapter you read. I would suggest that you schedule time to do your own study part (in 2-3 sittings) and not wait until the last-minute right before you are supposed to meet. If you race through it, you won't get very much out of it. I'd also suggest that you and your mentor be committed to the time(s) you schedule to meet, and try not to cancel/reschedule unless absolutely necessary. Take this seriously and it will be valuable. If you approach this half-heartedly, it will be a waste of time.

Got it? Great!

So, let's get started.

CHAPTER 1

Who Is God?

This study has to start with God. When you think about it, if there really is a God, ultimately, he is all that matters. God is the reason for everything and everyone. For us to understand life, our purpose, what the Bible is about, or just about anything else, we have to start with God, the creator and sovereign ruler over everything and everyone.

This book is actually an introductory study in theology. Don't let that word scare you. The word simply means "knowledge of God." And isn't that why we are doing this... to know more about God?

Knowing God is essential, not only for salvation or eternal life, but for spiritual growth and success in this life as well. Those who do not know God struggle through life without direction, answers and hope. But if God is the author of life, the best way to understand life is by first understanding who he is and what he is like.

In Psalm 46:10, the Lord says, *"Be still and know that I am God."* God wants us to know Him. But we have to be careful that we do not make the common mistake of dreaming up what we think God is like, or what we think he *should* be like. Instead, we need to find out what he says he is like. Our ideas about God need to be based on truth. What is he *really* like.

How can we find out who God is and what he is like?

Good question. We find out what God is like from two sources: General and Special Revelation.

The term, *revelation,* simply means, "what is revealed." In theology, we refer to revelation as things that God has revealed. Theologians speak of two ways that he does that and they use those terms.

General Revelation

General revelation is what God reveals about himself through his creation…the world he has created and the people he made in his image. It is the things that can be seen or known about God through creation and what is universally understood in the minds and consciences of people around the world. Theologians often say, "General revelation is found in creation and the conscience."

For example, the more we study this universe, the more we understand how huge it is, and how much power it contains. We also see that it is intricately organized, and that everything in it serves a purpose. This tells us some things about its creator, that he is obviously very powerful, if all the power in the universe came from him. We can see that he has an organized mind and that he is very purposeful in all that he does, even though we often will not understand his purpose in things.

By looking at the consciences of people that seem to be universal in history and around the world, we learn that ethics and morality matter to God. If our concept of right and wrong, justice and mercy, love, compassion, and even hatred, come from God, then we understand him to be moral and just, and that there are things he loves and things he despises.

Look up and read Psalm 19:1 and Romans 1:19-20; 2:14-15.

The heavens declare the glory of God; & the firmament sheweth his handy work. *because that which may be known of God is manifest in them; for God has shewed it unto them. For the invisible things of him*

Special Revelation

Special revelation, however, is more specific, like the label implies. It is defined as God's communication about specific things to specific people at specific times. While general revelation only reveals general things that are available to all people, special revelation is precise communication to an individual or group at a definite time and place.

Christians believe that God communicated directly with the writers of the sixty-six books of the Bible, and provided them with specific details, ideas, and guidelines that he wanted preserved for future generations.

That's how we believe we received the collection of writings that make up our Bible. Christians believe that the most accurate and reliable form of special revelation available to us is the Bible.

Because it is written down and preserved, it is traceable (we can find out who wrote it, where, and when), and testable (we can verify its data). For over two millennia, the books in the Bible have been studied, scrutinized, questioned and analyzed. If it were possible to find faults in it, by now, those would be glaring. But Christians like me, who are skeptical by nature, have been convinced that the books in the Bible are the most accurate documents in history.

If you are uncertain about the existence of God or doubt his personal interaction with his creation, or are suspicious about the credibility of the Bible, this is where you will become skeptical. But that's ok. We're not asking you to take the Bible as seriously as we do, yet. We believe that if God has spoken, he would want us to test and seek out evidence that would verify what was communicated as really being from Him. He is not against doubt. He just wants us to be fair with the evidence he gives us. He would not ask us to have blind faith in whatever anyone says. After all, anyone can *say* that they are a prophet of God. Christians are only supposed to listen to those who can substantiate that claim.

Our Source is The Bible

For this study, which is a "Bible study" we are going to be using the

Bible. While general revelation can be helpful with some things about God, it will take special revelation to really understand who God is and what his expectations of us are. Without special revelation, we would only be guessing. So, our source of learning in this chapter and all the subsequent chapters will be what God himself has said through his prophets, apostles, and of course, Jesus, as recorded in the Bible.

I'll be discussing more about the background and make-up of the Bible in chapter eight. But if you need convincing as to the general trustworthiness of the Bible, you may want to take a break from this study and first read *The Case for Christ* by Lee Strobel. It will be a good resource to help you see that there is no explanation for the Bible if it was not inspired by God.

Lee was an atheist who had been trained as a lawyer and was working for the Chicago Tribune as an award-winning journalist. When his wife became a Christian, it bothered him to the point that he considered ending the marriage. He went on a personal crusade to disprove the Bible and Christianity, but in his effort to discredit the Bible, he himself became convinced that it was true, and became a Christian. He is now very active at working to answer the objections of critics like himself.

Bear in mind that so much of what is said in popular media outlets regarding the Bible, come from an anti-supernatural mindset.

Whenever we approach a subject with a predisposition for or against anything, it makes it difficult to give the matter a fair hearing. When it comes to the Bible, because it addresses religious matters, and claims miraculous events in history, those with anti-supernatural presuppositions will naturally dismiss it. For many, since they reject the miracles of the Bible, their interpretation of its contents and approach to dating its writing (because of fulfilled prophecies) will be skewed by their predisposition.

On the other hand, scholars who approach the Bible believing that supernatural events are not necessarily impossible, see things differently. They are willing to weigh evidence that may corroborate a prophesy or something else that might be otherwise hard to believe.

So there are two schools of thought when it comes to the Bible. The one is more liberal and tends to be held by those who reject any supernatural activity in history. The other is more conservative and while very scholarly in its approach, differs from the liberal approach in that they accept the possibility of miracles. That might be an oversimplification, but it points out the differences in what many scholars believe regarding the Bible, and what you might see and hear on some public TV and popular history/science TV programs.

Many things that are in the Bible cannot be tested to prove that they are true. But many other things can be. What kind of evidence does the Bible contain within itself as far as its accuracy in the areas that can be tested? That's a good place to start if we are going to trust what it teaches about God. If what the Bible says in matters of history and geography can be demonstrated to be accurate, and if prophecies in the Bible can be shown to be fulfilled after their known date of proclamation, then we can know that it is a trustworthy book, and that at least some of the supernatural elements within it are plausible.

Much more will be said about the Bible, how we got it, how it is organized, and also about its reliability. But let's at least address some things that can help us know that the Bible has a high degree of accuracy. Perhaps more so than what you've been led to believe.

Accuracy and Trustworthiness of The Bible

The Bible is like no other book or collection of books in ancient or modern times. No documents of the ancient world compare. And no religious writings in history are anything like the Bible. Simply reading the Bible impresses the reader with its special character. While thousands of scrolls from the ancient world during the time the Bible was authored and collated have been found, none of them compare in character, accuracy, spiritual understanding and raw wisdom. Its character shows itself as being something very special.

Even when you compare the way miracles are recorded in the Bible with supernatural claims in other ancient writings, the Bible stands out uniquely. Other ancient works tell of crazy supernatural happenings that often make little sense, such as a woman with snakes for hair or a man with wings made of wax that melted when he flew too close to the sun. Ancient historians speak of the senseless nature of the supernatural claims made by ancients. But miracles in the Bible fulfilled a logical purpose. Yes, they were supernatural events, and that alone may make them hard to believe, but they made sense. Miracles enabled Israel to be freed from slavery and helped them settle the promised land. Jesus used miracles to feed hungry people and heal them of life-long ailments. They always had a reason.

Archeology

Certainly, not everything in the Bible can be tested. But a lot of things in the Bible can be. Hundreds of historical events are corroborated by non-Biblical sources. Geographical locations given in the Bible have been scrutinized and confirmed. Cultural practices spoken of in Scripture are validated by archeology. Everything in the Bible that can be tested has been. And time and again, the Bible being the most investigated collection of documents in history, also emerges as the most accurate.

The case of Sir William Ramsey is an interesting one. He had been trained at a university that had an anti-Bible bias, and began his career as an archeologist and historian in the early 20th century. When he began his career, he believed that the New Testament book of Acts was a 2nd-3rd century synthesis of Christian writers, based on legends, and that its historicity and geography could not be trusted. At one point he called it, "a highly imaginative and carefully colored account of primitive Christianity."

But after decades of archeological research, and having become a world renown and leading archeologist of ancient Greece and Asia Minor (modern Turkey), he reversed his earlier view and concluded that Luke was indeed the author of Acts and that it was authored in the first century. He stated that it was the most accurate geographical tool ever tested. In *The*

Bearing of Recent Discoveries on the Trustworthiness of the New Testament, he wrote:

> *"Further study . . . showed that the book could bear the most minute scrutiny as an authority for the facts of the Aegean world, and that it was written with such judgment, skill, art and perception of truth as to be a model of historical statement."*

Ramsey went on in his career to put the epistles of Paul to archeological and historical tests, and later wrote extensively on his reasons for believing that all 13 of the epistles that claim to be written by Paul, were in fact, and contained the same degree of accuracy as the Book of Acts. In one of his last public statements he disparaged modern critical New Testament scholarship as being governed by biased anti-supernatural presuppositions. He went on to claim that true scientific research on the accuracy of the New Testament text leads students to recognize that in the areas the New Testament can be investigated, it is found to be true.

William Albright was an equally respected archeologist of the mid 20th century. His work focused on examining the pre-Christian or Old Testament world. His story is similar to William Ramsey's. He too had been trained to believe that the Old Testament timeline of events was fabricated, and that the stories were myths and legends. But after becoming the 20th century's leading archeologist, his work had changed his mind, and today he is known as the architect of Biblical archeology. Because he found archeology to substantiate what is written in the Bible, he put forth strong arguments for its veracity.

Perhaps the most well-known authority on modern archeology of the 20th century is Dr. Nelson Glueck, a Jewish archeologist. He said this:

> *"No archeological discovery has ever controverted a Biblical reference. Scores of archeological findings have been made which confirm in clear outline or in exact detail historical statements in the Bible. And, by the same token, proper evaluation of Biblical descriptions has often led to amazing discoveries."*
> *–Nelson Glueck, Rivers in the Desert: History of Negev*

Fulfilled Prophecy

Archeology is not the only means to test the accuracy or trustworthiness of the Bible. Fulfilled prophecy is another. The manner in which prophets predicted future events in great detail, and how those events actually occurred, led secularists (those who dismiss God's involvement in history) to conclude that prophetic passages had to have been written after the prophesied events, and only *claimed* to be prophetic. But time and again, with the discovery of earlier manuscripts or other validation of what was written, the passages were proven to be authentic.

I'll give just a couple of examples.

In Daniel 9:24-27, Daniel predicts a soon-to-be decree allowing Jews to return to Jerusalem. He then goes on to claim that 69 weeks later (a week in Daniel's day is any group of 7, as a dozen is a group of 12), the Messiah would come, and would be put to death. When you calculate the decree by Cyrus to release the Jews back to their homeland out 483 years, that brings us to 28 AD, based on our best estimates and calculations of the three ancient calendars (Persian, Jewish and Roman). Almost all scholars agree that Jesus was crucified somewhere in the neighborhood of 30 AD. When you consider the rounded off numbers used for these years (weeks of years), this is an accurate prediction of Jesus' crucifixion. It is such a remarkable prophecy that nineteenth century liberal scholars claimed it had to have been a post-Christian addition to Daniel's book. But today, after pre-Christian copies of that prophecy have been found, identical to the later copies that had been rejected, all agree, it was, in fact, written long before Jesus was alive.

Another example is found in Psalm 22:12-18. Psalm 22 is a "Messianic Psalm," meaning that it was a prophecy regarding the Messiah. It paralleled a later Messianic Prophecy, Isaiah 53, in that it foretold the suffering and death of the coming Messiah. What is interesting about Psalm 22 is that it describes in detail what a crucifixion victim would experience.

Crucifixion was a horrible method of execution that ancients used on their most odious criminals. The victim would be hung on a wooden stake with arms outstretched, fastened to a crosspiece attached to the stake. They would eventually die in the elements, often after hanging for days. It is the only form of ancient execution that could be described the way the Messiah's death was predicted in Psalm 22.

But here's the thing, crucifixion had not been invented yet when Psalm 22 was written. The Babylonians came up with the first form of crucifixion hundreds of years later. The Romans got it from the Babylonians and perfected it as an even slower and more torturous death.

Hundreds of years before it was ever practiced, the Psalmist spoke of it in detail, predicting it to be experienced by the Messiah.

Again, this was a remarkable prophecy, so much so that liberal scholars tried to insist that the text itself was later changed by Christians to make it sound more like the crucifixion of Jesus. However, it was not long before much earlier Hebrew manuscripts, such as the Dead Sea scrolls, which predate Jesus, as well as pre-Christian translations of the passage, verified the text as it appears in our modern English Bibles.

Those are just two prophecies that were undoubtedly fulfilled in a remarkable way. But there are over 350 prophecies of the Messiah that were fulfilled by Jesus! Peter Stoner, in his acclaimed work, *Science Speaks*, calculated the mathematical probability of all the prophecies regarding the Messiah to be fulfilled by chance as $1/10^{157}$. That's a 1 with 157 zeros after it! We are talking about unfathomable odds!

Scientific Insight

The Bible is certainly not a science text book. It was not written to teach us about the intricacies of the universe or explain natural phenomena. But where it does speak to scientific matters, it demonstrates remarkable insight.

For example, in Isaiah 40:22, the prophet says, "It is he (God) who sits above the circle of the earth…" The Hebrew word translated "circle" literally means, "roundness." Isaiah refers to the Lord as sitting above the roundness of the earth, in a time when only a few obscure Greek philosophers speculated the possible shape of the earth to be spherical. Instead, in popular culture of the day, the prevailing view was that the earth was flat. But that's not what Isaiah believed.

Dr. Henry Morris listed some of the statements in Scripture that speak of knowledge that the human authors would not have had on their own in that day regarding scientific truths that we know today. Here are some of them:

- Almost infinite extent of the celestial universe (Isaiah 55:9)
- Law of conservation of mass and energy (II Peter 3:7)
- Hydrologic cycle (Ecclesiastes 1:7)
- Vast number of stars (Jeremiah 33:22)
- Law of increasing entropy (degeneration) (Psalm 102:25-27)
- Paramount importance of blood in life processes (Leviticus 17:11)
- Atmospheric circulation (Ecclesiastes 1:6)
- Gravitational field (Job 26:7)

These insights should not be misunderstood. I'm not saying that the Bible should replace our science books in school, or that God gave us the Scriptures so that we do not further our understanding of his creation and explore, examine and debate using scientific inquiry. But the knowledge displayed in the Scriptures speak of a scientific accuracy that does not seem appropriate for ancient people to have conceived on their own. It seems apparent that there was divine intervention in producing these observations.

Once again, when you compare the Bible to other ancient documents, there is nothing like it. No other book was authored by so many people, from such a vast array of backgrounds, writing about so many controversial topics, and all the while agreeing with one another in every way. The unity, diversity, morality, character, insight and accuracy of the Bible set it apart from all other ancient documents.

This uniqueness of the Bible is also apparent when it is compared to later religious writings, such as the Koran and the Book of Mormon, both of which contain known geographical, grammatical, historical and scientific errors.

To give just a couple of examples, the Koran claims that human beings are created from a drop of liquid (presumably sperm) that is formed in a man's chest. But we now know that sperm is formed below the lower abdomen in the testicles.

The Koran also speaks of Samaritans during the time of Moses, though Samaritans did not become a people group until the Babylonian Captivity, which took place hundreds of years after Moses.

The Book of Mormon speaks of animals existing in North America in a time long before they existed on the continent (honey bees, horses, and elephants) and talks about materials (silk and steel) supposedly being in ancient Israel centuries before they actually were. It also claims that modern Native Americans were of middle eastern descent. DNA testing has proven that to also not be true.

While there have been challenges to the truthfulness of statements in the Bible, even those challenges stand out in stark contrast to other religious documents that claim similar authority. The Bible has proven itself effective in standing up to scrutiny.

These paragraphs are certainly not exhaustive proofs as to the accuracy of everything in the Bible. So much more has been written by qualified people with respected credentials in ancient history. But I hope this helps you to have at least a high regard for what is written in the Bible, and that you are willing to trust its credibility in what it says regarding spiritual matters.

Christians look to and trust the Bible as Special Revelation that gives us specific information about God, the world he created, humanity and our essential problem, as well as how we can know and relate to God.

Back to who God is…

For this study, we are going to look at what God says about himself in Scripture.

In order for us to get to know who he is and what he is like, we have to first lay aside our presuppositions and possible misconceptions about him and instead adjust our thoughts of what God is like to what he says about himself. After all, this is too weighty of a matter to rely on speculations and imaginations that have no basis in fact. Rather than guessing what God is like, let's look to the source that has proven itself to be reliable and trustworthy and claims to have accurate information on who he is and what he is like.

So, then, Who is God? What is He Like?

He is the **creator** of **everything!**

When studying God, this is a logical place to begin. Consider it. If God made absolutely everything; if he brought matter and energy into existence, every molecule, every atom, extending to the far reaches of the universe; if he made it all, there are some major ramifications to this! And the Bible does unequivocally say that God did make everything.

Let's just look at two places. First, the opening words in Genesis (which means "Beginnings").

Read Genesis 1:1 and summarize it.

The New Testament also affirms this. Read Acts 17:24 and summarize it.

So that's what the Bible says. But you already knew that, didn't you?

It wasn't that long ago when knowing and believing that God is the creator of everything was nearly universal. But much has changed in this generation alone. People watch the Discovery Channel and hear academics claim that the existence of the universe can be explained with mathematics. We are inundated with the message that God is not needed any longer to explain how things came to be. Science has solved the problem. And some want to say that science has eliminated the need for religious belief.

Does science contradict God? Should Christians feel threatened by science?

Read Psalm 19:1 again. Remember what it says? Write the verse out here:

Science means "knowledge." Science is simply the study of what is in existence. It does not seek answers as to "why" something is in existence. That would be philosophy. Science engages in the process of learning everything possible about whatever is being studied.

In Psalm 19, King David, the writer of this Psalm, was saying that science declares God's glory. The more we learn about this universe, the bigger and smarter and more powerful God emerges in our minds.

So, science does not contradict God, it celebrates him!

But there are some problems with science. Science is merely a field of study that focuses on measuring, testing and proving. However, not everything can be measured, tested, or proven. The scientific method involves making hypotheses and with a level of evidence, multiple theories are developed until one of them is proven to be true. The nature of science is that new theories are continually postulated and tested until one becomes dominant due to the evidence. Older theories that had been accepted prior, are regularly replaced when newer theories, that better fits the evidence, are developed. It's why a number of scientists speak of science being wrong, regularly, and how that is a good thing.

The problem is, some scientific theories are often taught or presented in popular media, as fact, when nothing has been proven. Many of the supposed scientific facts that people believe today are still very much theoretical, but passed along as fact. That's why many past "scientific facts" have since been disproved (i.e. spontaneous generation, alchemy, Einstein's static universe, cold fusion). Many things that were taught to be true in the past, have since been deemed "misunderstood" and later debunked. Who's to say that what is accepted as scientific fact today will not be rejected in a few decades? This is a matter that many secular scientists and philosophers are beginning to talk about (i.e. *But What If We're Wrong?* by Chuck Klosterman and *Why Science is Wrong...: About Almost Everything* by Alex Tsakiris).

If course, what comes to mind is the theory of evolution. Atheists and agnostics hang their hat on this theory as an explanation for the natural world without God.

While I don't want to get into details of the creation/evolution debate in this book, evolutionary theory does not explain the existence of matter, energy, or the genesis of life. In fact, secular scientists are hard pressed to even come up with an adequate definition of life, much less to be able to explain how it could possibly have self-generated. In recent years, a number of biologists have come forward to question the validity of accepted evolutionary theory because of the unexplained gaps in the evidence that is supposed to support it (see *Darwin's Doubt* by Stephen C. Meyer). They complain that rather than addressing the weaknesses of some aspects of evolution because of lack of evidence, many evolutionists simply ignore the holes.

My contention is that naturalism (belief that the universe can be explained entirely by natural causes) requires at least as much faith to believe as does theistic creation (that God created the universe). In that sense, science moves from knowledge to philosophy and for some, it has essentially become their religion.

Yet, many scientists are believers in God. A 2005 Rice University study found that despite far greater occupational pressure to the contrary than most other careers, two thirds of all scientists believe in God.

Louis Agassiz, probably the most famous natural scientist in history, said this:

> *"In our study of natural objects, we are approaching the thoughts of the Creator, reading his conceptions, interpreting a system that is his and not ours" (Methods of Study in Natural History).*

In other words, Agassiz was agreeing with King David. Scientific knowledge declares God's glory. It does not detract from it.

If we are honest, we'd have to admit, there are no adequate explanations for the universe or for life apart from Genesis 1:1.

God is the creator of everything in existence.

What should we learn from that? Well first, there is a God, and he made you and everything around you. If he made it all, including us, we owe not just our lives to him, but our very existence. He made everything, and by that, he *owns* everything.

So, the first thing we know about God is that he is real, and he is the maker of everything. That includes you. He made you and everything around you. We would not be in existence if it were not for him.

He is the **sustainer** of **everything!**

God not only made everything, he keeps it all in existence. If it were not for God's active involvement in what he created, it would cease to exist. He perpetuates creation.

Read Colossians 1:17 and then Hebrews 1:3. Where in these verses do you find this concept?

These two verses above were originally written in Greek and translated for us into English. Sometimes it helps us to get a deeper understanding of what was written by going back to its original. This is true for both of these passages.

Colossians 1:17 says that in Jesus, all things "hold together" (ESV). That's a good translation. "Hold together" is a single Greek word (sunesteken) that Paul, the author, put together from two words to give the sense of the world being "kept together." It is an active verb, meaning, it is something that God continues to do. He *is* holding the world together.

Albert Einstein, believed by some to be the most intelligent genius of modern times, spent the latter half of his life searching for what he called, "the secret of the universe," something he never found. Einstein noted that physicists understand a lot of things about gravity and the nature of subatomic activity, but they know nothing of what causes it all. They know that there is a relationship between density, mass, and gravitational force, but they don't know why there is that relationship, what the root cause is. They understand many things about atoms, electrons, protons, and neutrons. But they do not know what keeps atoms together, what the attraction is between its parts that keeps not only the atoms, but also the materials the atoms form, in existence. While they harness and utilize the power of magnetism, so much about it is a complete mystery. If whatever force that holds these things in existence were to be neutralized, everything would disintegrate. What is that force? Einstein died not knowing.

But we do. "In him all things hold together" (Colossians 1:17). God is actively sustaining all things. He is the force that brought it into existence, and he is the force that keeps it all together and functioning the way he designed it.

Here's what Einstein said:

> *"Everyone who is seriously involved in the pursuit of science becomes convinced that a spirit is manifest in the laws of the universe - a spirit vastly superior to that of man, and one in the face of which we with our modest powers must feel humble. In this way the pursuit of science leads to a religious feeling of a special sort, which is indeed quite different from the religiosity of someone more naive."*

God is not only the creator of all that there is, he is the sustainer of all that there is.

Hebrews 1:3 tells us the same thing. The Greek word for "upholds" (pherōn) means, "keeps it going." In its Greek form, it is a present active participle, meaning that God's creation was not just a one-time act, it is something he actively sustains.

So, God is not just a superhuman watchmaker who made the universe and wound it up to let it go. He actively maintains the universe and sustains its very existence. Everything owes its existence to God and is continually dependent on him.

What do we learn about God from this? Well, not only did God make you and everything around you, he keeps you and everything around you going. In other words, if he didn't want you to be here, you wouldn't be. You are alive because God wants you to be.

That should tell you something about him!

He is **One** in **Three** Persons (Trinity)

In both the Old Testament and the New Testament, all of the human authors undoubtedly believed and proclaimed that there was one God and only one God. That stood in stark contrast to the religious beliefs around the world. For thousands of years, only the Jews believed in just one God (some identify Zoroastrianism from Persia as an exception, but it was not truly monotheistic). Even in the early Christian era, only Christians and Jews held to a belief in one God. It set them apart from all other religious systems. But it was foundational to their beliefs and they proclaimed it without apology.

Look up Deuteronomy 6:4 and 1 Timothy 2:5. Write out the phrase from each verse that proclaims there to be only one God:

While the Bible universally proclaims there to be one God, there are a number of places in the Old Testament where it appears that there is a plural dimension to this one God.

Read Genesis 1:26. Is the word for "God" here plural or singular?

Are the pronouns that refer to God plural or singular?

Read Isaiah 6:8. God is talking. What do you see in his use of pronouns referring to himself?

So there seems to be an implied plural dimension to this one God in the Old Testament.

Then, in the New Testament, three persons in the Bible are said to be God: the Father, the Son (Jesus), and the Holy Spirit. Look up the following texts and answer the questions.

Matthew 6:26, 30, 32 – Who does Jesus refer to as "God" in this passage?

John 1:1 – Who does the Apostle John say is God in this verse?

Acts 5:3-4 – Who does Peter say that Ananias lied to in v. 3?

Who does he say he lied to in v. 4?

So then, who is Peter saying is God in this passage?

As you can see in the Scriptures you just looked up, the Bible teaches that there is only one God, but that there is a plural dimension to this one God. The New Testament teaches that the Father is God, and that Jesus is

God, and that The Holy Spirit is God.

How can that be?

One God, three persons. It's not something that we can fully grasp or understand, but we can believe.

The Christian Scriptures teach that there is one God, but he is three distinct persons. He is a triune God. The Trinity.

CHAPTER 2

What Is He Like?

What is God like?

In our last chapter, we began to explore who God is. We learned that he is the creator and sustainer of everything, including us. And we learned that he exists as a triune God: one God in three persons.

But what is he like? That's what this chapter is about. Hopefully, we'll learn some things that will help us discover not only some important things about him, but that those truths will help us understand ourselves and where we fit in.

He is very different from us

God is our creator, we are his creation. That alone sets him far apart from us. As our creator, he is so far beyond us that we cannot expect to fully comprehend him.

God can completely understand us, but we will never be able to fully comprehend him or understand his actions. He's just too far beyond us. And when you think about it, it's quite presumptuous of us to think that we can.

Read Isaiah 55:9 and write out what God says about this:

I love the story told of the church father Augustine while he was in the middle of a lengthy theological treatise on the Trinity. His head was swimming and he took a break by walking along the sea. He noticed a little boy who had dug a hole and was running back and forth carrying water in a seashell from the sea to his hole. Augustine asked, "What are you doing, lad?"

The boy replied, "I'm going to empty the sea into my hole." Augustine chuckled to himself, thinking how silly and impossible that would be.

But then Augustine realized that was what he was attempting to do with God. He was trying to bring all of the depth and intricacies and might of who God is into his tiny little brain. It could never be done.

God is vastly beyond us, in power and comprehension and almost every other way. We should learn everything we can about him, but we will never be in a position to make judgments on him or expect to understand all of his ways. He is too far beyond us.

God is Great!

What is it about God that makes him so far beyond us?

When theologians talk about what God is like, they use the term "attributes" and divide up the characteristics of God between his "transferrable attributes" and "non-transferable attributes." That's an elaborate way to distinguish between the characteristics of God that he shares with us, or infused in our make-up, and those that are true only of him.

It's his non-transferrable attributes that make him far beyond us. These are the attributes that identify him as great. Later in the chapter, we'll examine the attributes that display his goodness. But first, let's see what it is about him that shows his greatness.

He is **sovereign**

Look up Psalm 103:19 and Isaiah 40:21-26 and write what the authors say about God in these passages.

When we say that God is sovereign, we mean that he is in absolute control over everything that he wants to control. Nothing happens that is beyond his command.

He never says, "Uh-oh."

He is **eternal**

God has no beginning and will have no ending.

This is a tough one for us to fathom. It's one of those things that used to keep many of us awake at night when we were kids. How could God just always be? Everything in our experience has a beginning. How could God not have a beginning?

But having a beginning doesn't make it easier to understand. After all, how *could* God have a beginning?

The best way to think of this is to recognize time as an aspect of his creation. God created time as a mechanism to organize events chronologically. But it's not a boundary for God. He exists outside of any boundaries, any constraints, even time. He lives in eternity. His perspective is not restricted by occasion.

So, God is not limited by time. He is outside of it. Time is something he created, not something that he is subservient to.

That's the essence of these "greatness attributes." They show God to be beyond any limitation.

It's just that time is something that is so basic to our understanding of existence that we can't comprehend anything without it. But God can. We need time. God doesn't.

I know, it's still not something we can entirely grasp. It's one of those things that is beyond our ability to fit into small finite brains. Not just yours, mine too.

But nevertheless, God is eternal. Psalm 9:7, Isaiah 57:15 and 1 Timothy 1:17 are just a few Scriptures that refer to God as eternal. Look them up. Genesis 1 opens with God in full power, and Revelation closes with God in full power. He has no beginning and no ending. He is not limited by time. He is eternal.

He is **omniscient**

Sorry, I could've just said, "all-knowing." But then you wouldn't have been impressed with my knowledge of Latin. (I did take a year of it in high school.)

Look up Psalm 139:1-6 and Hebrews 4:13 and write what these verses say about God and what he knows.

There isn't anything that can be known that God does not know. He has all knowledge that there is to have. He never needs to learn anything new. He doesn't have to study, or stop to remember. Nothing ever takes him by surprise. He knows everything that there is to know.

He is all-knowing.

He is **all-powerful**

The theologians say, "omnipotent," but again, that's just Latin for "all-powerful."

Write what the following verses say about God's power:

Jeremiah 32:17, 27

Psalm 147:5

Hebrews 1:3

This is the one attribute of God that I think most people get. After all, he's God. He's that powerful. He created the universe and we know that it's really big and there's a lot of power in it, so he's got to be pretty powerful himself!

In fact, all the power of the universe is contained within God and it emanates from his being. He has never been and never will be limited by a lack of strength or ability. All strength and ability flows from him, so all power comes from him.

He is **everywhere**

The theme we have so far is that God is limitless. He is not limited by time or lacking knowledge or strength. He is also not limited by space or place. That is what theologians mean by "omni-presence." There is no place where God is not in some sense, present. Everything and every place is in existence because he brought it into existence and keeps it in existence. There is no place where he is forbidden or kept away from. There is no place where he is not. God is everywhere.

Look up Psalm 139:7-12 and Proverbs 15:3 and write what they say about the presence of God:

He is **unchanging**

What do Malachi 3:6 and Hebrews 13:8 say about God?

God is immutable, or unchanging in His nature and in his ultimate purpose. He is constant. He has always been and always will be fully God, in complete possession of all His attributes. He has no need to learn and grow, because he has always been fully God, limitless, and perfect.

By this we do not mean sterile or immobile. God is dynamic, active, and involved—but he is stable and dependable. And he is faithful and trustworthy.

So, in many ways, God is very different from us. He would have to be, to be our creator. If he is the Maker and we are his creation, of course we could never be at his level or be just like him.

And yet, it may surprise you to find out that in many ways, he is a lot like us. And in many other ways, he wants us to be more like him.

Keep reading.

He is a lot like us!

Believe it or not, in a lot of ways, God is like us. We have many characteristics that he shared with us. What are those traits?

He has a **mind, will** and **emotions**

Like us, he has a mind (self-awareness and logical thinking), will (moral and ethical decision-making) and emotions (feelings and empathy for others).

Look up the following verses and record what this says about what God is like.

Mind
Psalm 139:17

Isaiah 55:8-9

Will
Genesis 1:26

John 6:40

Emotions
Psalm 103:13

Isaiah 62:5

Knowing that God thinks, makes decisions, and feels emotion, how does that affect what you think about God?

He has **plans** and **purposes**

He also makes plans and has a purpose for why he does things. Look up the following verses and write what they say about this.

Jeremiah 29:11

Romans 8:28

What do these verses tell us about the universe, our lives, and everything that happens?

He is **relational**

While many of us need some alone time, all of us crave friendship and relationships. We got that from God. In fact, we will learn in the next chapter, that's the reason he created us, to enjoy a relationship with us.

God is relational. In the very beginning in Genesis chapter one, we learn that God enjoyed fellowship within the Trinity even before we were created. Our ability to relate with one another and have friendships is a characteristic of his that he shared with us

Read John 15:9 and James 2:23 and write out what we learn about God in these passages.

We were patterned after him (created in his image)

Before we talk about this, read Genesis 1:26-27, and write down some of the things from those two verses that stand out about God and how he created us.

Besides the plural pronouns that we talked about in the last chapter, the part I want you to notice here is where God decides to make people in his image, after his likeness.

Of course, it doesn't mean physically. God isn't physical, he's spiritual (John 4:24). He isn't limited by a physical body. But this passage says that God made us after his likeness, in his image. We'll discuss this more in the next chapter, but we learn from this that in many ways, we can relate to God. We have many of his relatable characteristics, and we were given a soul. This was never said of anything else that was created...plant or animal life. Only people.

Being created with a soul in God's image means that we were created with the ability to know and love on a spiritual level, to be able to relate with Him and others created after his image. It means that we've been created as moral creatures, with the ability to choose good or evil, that we have a free will to choose or reject a relationship with him. And the essence of who we are is not limited to our physical bodies, but extends beyond our physical lives on earth.

Being created in God's image also speaks of our potential to reflect his transferable attributes.

I already mentioned God's "transferable attributes." And we've talked about a couple of them, that all people exhibit: mind, will, emotions, plans, purposes, and being relational.

There are some other transferable attributes that are part of God's makeup, that we don't all necessarily have. But he offers them to us. These are attributes that involve God's goodness. Being "godly" means to exhibit these "godlike" characteristics: holiness, righteousness, justice, truth, and love. Let's take a brief look at them.

God is Good!

He is **Holy**

Look up Exodus 15:11 and Psalm 99:9 and write a brief synopsis of what you see in these verses.

God is absolutely holy. There is no flaw in him or in what he does. He is the one who sets the standard of what is right and wrong. It's his universe and his laws. Therefore, he always does what is right. It's part of what makes him a good God.

He is **Righteous** and **Just**

Read Psalm 45:6 and write what you see in this verse.

By this we mean that his actions and judgments are consistent with his holiness. There is perfect fidelity between what he declares to be right and what he does. He rules and judges the universe justly, in harmony with his holiness. If he didn't, he wouldn't be good. But because he is good, he is holy, righteous and just.

He is **Truth**

What do Deuteronomy 32:4 and Psalm 31:5 tell us about God?

Everything about God is truthful. He always tells the truth. He can never lie. Whatever he says is true. He is always right. And he puts on no pretense but is exactly who He says He is. He tells the truth and he conducts himself in truth.

He is **Love**

This one we love to talk about. Jesus' closest friend, John, said that love defines God, and that none of us can be in fellowship with him if we do not act in, and practice, love.

Look up these verses also and note what it says about God's love: John 3:16; Romans 5:8: 2 Corinthians 5:21

So much more is said in Scripture regarding God's love that we could never touch on all of it here. But it is clear that he relates to his creation with compassion, care and a willingness to sacrifice in order to do so.

His love is unconditional. It's not based on our merit or any "loveliness" of those He loves. He loves us just because he does.

When my children were small, I would often ask them, "Why do I love you so much?" And they would answer, "Because you are my daddy."

We had taught them from an early age that we loved them no matter what. Even though they may do wrong and we may sometimes be disappointed in their misbehavior, we taught our children that they could do nothing to make us love them more, or less.

And that's the kind of love God has for us. He loves us just because he does and his love is not based on our merit. It's unconditional love.

Aspects of God's love include grace, mercy and patience.

Grace means "undeserved gift." It is because of God's grace that we are given so much. We haven't earned his blessing. He is good to us because of who he is, not because we are so deserving.

Mercy means withholding deserved punishment. God's love for us provides mercy. Though we turn away from him, often ignore him, and sometimes openly rebel against him, he is merciful to us.

While his righteousness and justice must be satisfied (or he would not be good), because of his love for us, he is patient and waiting for our repentance. It's his love that brought about the greatest sacrifice ever, and which satisfies his justice and provides for our way back to him.

Because God desires a reciprocal loving relationship with us, and because his love for us is genuine, he honors us, the objects of his love, with the freedom to choose whether or not we will love Him back.

CHAPTER 3

Who Are You?

W ho am I? Why am I here? What, if any, is the meaning of life? People have been plagued with these questions throughout all history. If this study will achieve anything, it must answer these questions.

So, while we needed to start our study with God, we can't ignore our own condition. Now we need to tackle the questions of humanity before we can see how these two subjects (theology and anthropology) intersect.

Studying anthropology is studying a collection of paradoxes. On the one hand, people are resourceful, ingenious, and adept at manipulating what is around them to create a pleasant and enjoyable atmosphere. Think of what accomplished pianists can do with artfully crafted wood and iron at their fingertips. On the other hand, think of what others do with the same materials, wood and iron, fashioned into weapons of destruction. As Stuart Briscoe once said, "Man can tame the wilds, but not his temper. He drills for oil from beneath frozen wasteland and uses it to run engines made from materials he mined in other parts of the world, but then fills the air he breathes with fumes from the oil he burns." These contradictions make up the "mystery of humanity."

This is probably why philosophers from all cultures and in all ages have asked the question that the Psalmist asked in Psalm 8:4, "What is man?"

So then... *Who are you?*

Why are you here?

How can your life take on meaning and significance?

The World Gets It Wrong

If you talk to the average anthropologist, sociologist, or psychologist, you will hear how human beings are highly evolved animals. We can reason better, communicate more precisely, fashion and use tools and plan for the future. But we're still only higher forms of mammals.

People are animals

This was a foreign concept to people around the world until the late nineteenth century when Charles Darwin began publishing his theories of evolution and naturalism. Darwin began promoting his theories as a study in how God created life forms, but his views were picked up and quickly developed into a quest to eliminate God altogether from science. We discussed this briefly in chapter one and there are many good works written by men of science and deep faith that may be helpful. But the result of Darwinian naturalism is the popular view that people are merely animals. Nothing more.

Twentieth century psychologists added to this animalizing of humanity. Sigmund Freud reduced human anxiety to the struggle against raw sexual drives in order to appease cultural expectations. Behaviorists, such as Skinner and Pavlov, viewed human free will as simply the outcomes of behavioral conditioning, that there is no real free will, after all. They denied any immaterial or spiritual part of human beings. Even the mind was said to be only biological functions reacting to a mechanical universe that makes us think and do the things we do.

A number of years ago, a popular daytime talk show host, Phil Donahue, wrote and published a book titled, *The Human Animal*. Shortly after, he did a series of shows on teenage suicide and invited several teenagers who had attempted suicide themselves, onto the program.

One guest was a friend of mine. Her name was Holly Flagg and she had become a Christian shortly after her last of several suicide attempts. By the time she was on the program, her life had changed dramatically and she was a happy young woman who was then involved in helping other young women to come to the place that she had. On live television, Donahue asked her, "Why would a teenager want to end her life?"

She responded with poise and grace, "If your life is a major struggle, and you've been taught that we are only animals anyway, there doesn't seem to be any reason to go on living." The author of *The Human Animal* quickly moved his microphone to the next young person.

But Holly was right. Is that really all we are? A highly evolved biological mechanism, brought into existence by the random activities of a chance universe? A view like that can lead to some serious despondency. Talk about hopelessness and despair!

People are accidental and temporary products of the universe

Here's how one well-known atheist philosopher, Bertrand Russel, who believed just that, described his inner feelings that were the result of his understanding of who he really was:

> *"Brief and powerless is Man's life; on him and all his race the slow, sure doom falls pitiless and dark. Blind to good and evil, reckless of destruction, omnipotent matter rolls on its relentless way; for Man, condemned today to lose his dearest, tomorrow himself to pass through the gate of darkness, it remains only to cherish, ere yet the blow falls, the lofty thought that ennoble his little day; ... proudly defiant of the irresistible forces that tolerate, for a moment, his knowledge and his condemnation, to sustain alone, a weary but unyielding Atlas, the world that his own ideals have fashioned despite the trampling march of unconscious power."*
> *–Bertrand Russell (A Free Man's Worship)*

This is the view that people are accidental and temporary products of the universe. Man is a hopeless result of natural causes, about to be crushed into oblivion by the same causes.

Are you inspired?

There are other erroneous views that the secular world has of humanity.

People are sexual, material or economic entities

For many, people are just tools for their own purposes. They are sexual, material or economic entities, whose worth is only based on what value they bring to others. Why do some corporations take advantage of their work force and use and dispense with people as though they were material goods? Why else is there a porn industry that is thriving? Why is human trafficking the international crisis that it is? Because for many, people are merely material, sexual, or economic entities with no intrinsic value.

People are free beings

Another prominent view of humanity is that people are absolutely free beings, with no obligation or responsibility to a higher being or a creator. This view is more prominent in America than most other places around the world. For those who champion it, the highest good and personal achievement to be pursued is to be absolutely free.

Free from any control.
Free from any authority.
Free from any accountability.

Take, for example, the 90s box office hit, *The Truman Show*, starring Jim Carrey. Carrey played a key figure in a reality show. He was, in fact,

Truman, the subject of the show, *The Truman Show*. He was also the only person on the show who did not know that he was on TV. The TV set was his life. He was born on the set and from his birth, hidden cameras surrounded him, recording everything, his childhood, teenage years, and early adult life. The world watched as he learned to talk, walk, go to school, enjoy his first date, and get married. Truman thought that everything around him was real, and to him, the people around him were his family and friends. But they were all just actors and his hometown, job, etc., were all part of the set for his reality TV show, *The Truman Show*. Even his wife was an actress and part of the charade. In the movie, Truman eventually figured out the truth...that he didn't really have his own life, but that his surroundings were controlled by someone else out there, producing and directing the TV show. He attempted to escape but the directors used supposed life events to bring him back. But it was too late and the show culminated with a conversation between Truman and the reality show's producer.

A booming voice came over the set addressing Truman, who then asked, "Who are you?"

"I am your creator."

The message from the movie was obvious. While the producer was not a bad person in the movie. He seemed to really care about Truman. But he had no right to control his life the way he did. Truman was his own man and should be free from the control of those who were orchestrating his life and using it for entertainment and personal gain.

That is true. After all, the program's producer and directors were all just men like Truman was. The producer had no right to control Truman. But the analogy in the movie seemed directed at God as mankind's creator. As though God may be good and powerful, but he does not have a right to dictate to us, and we are not ultimately responsible to anyone, even our creator.

And that's also where the analogy breaks down. The TV producer wasn't really Truman's creator. He was just a man. He was Truman's equal.

God, however, is God. He is the reason for our existence. And his pleasure is the purpose for our existence. He made us for himself. He is the creator and sustainer of all things, including our lives. If he were to withdraw his support for a second, we would cease to exist.

The truth is, none of us are absolutely free. While God gives us the ability to choose right and wrong, to follow him or rebel, we are all totally dependent on him and accountable to him. We are free in a sense, but we are not absolutely free. We are finite and dependent creatures. Only God is fully autonomous. Only God is absolutely free.

People are gods

A view of mankind that is related to this declares that every person is entirely responsible for their own destiny. Because we are autonomous beings, free and dependent and accountable to no one, it is up to us to make our own way and create significance in life.

William Ernest Henley wrote these famous poetic words many years ago:

Out of the night that covers me,
Black as the Pit from pole to pole,
I thank whatever gods may be for my unconquerable soul...
It matters not how strait the gate,
How charged with punishments the scroll,
I am the master of my fate; I am the captain of my soul.

Henley fell into the same trap that people of all ages and in all places have been tempted to fall into, baited by the same lie the serpent brought to Eve in the Garden of Eden in Genesis 3, that people can be their own gods. There is no need for a sovereign God that we are accountable to. We can arrange our own lives, the people and things around us, for our own benefit, live life for our own selves, as though we are the centers of our own worlds. We can be our own gods!

And everywhere you look, you see people living that way. In essence, it's the definition of sin. Turning away from the one true God, denying accountability to him, and doing as we please, instead of as he pleases. We try to be our own little gods.

There's Something Awry

As with all error that catches on, there is some truth in some of these erroneous views of mankind. People have some similarities to animals (we have a mutual designer and creator). Other people can and should to some degree add value to us, and we to them. People have been given a certain level of freedom by God, and we are responsible for the choices we make in life. But individually and collectively, there are serious flaws with these false views of humanity.

And let's face it, after everything has been tried and many have attempted to live by every philosophy that ignores God, these views do not fit the reality of our human experience.

Even a zoologist does not view his own newborn child as just another mammal.

We know that animals, no matter how intelligent, do not ponder philosophical or spiritual concepts. Animals do not consider "the meaning of life." They do not possess a self-awareness that people do. That's not an issue with intelligence, it's an issue of essence...what they are and who we are.

There is a spiritual dimension to our existence, something every person in every culture around the world in all ages has possessed. We know intrinsically that we are not merely animals. We have a yearning for the spiritual, something that cannot be explained through naturalism.

And here's something else to consider, *when the supposed fundamental needs of secular views of humanity are satisfied, emptiness and dissatisfaction remain.* Any view of humanity that misses the significance of who created us, and why we were created, will eventually lead to that inner emptiness and dissatisfaction.

Who Are We, Really?

But there is an alternative. In the Bible, we are told who we are and why we were created. Getting this understanding helps us to become everything we were meant to be and to enjoy the ultimate of fulfillment in life.

Look up Genesis 1:26-28 and answer these questions from the text.

Who wanted people to be in existence in the first place?

Who decided what people would look like and be like?

Who created people?

What is different about the way we were created (as opposed to animals)?

Fill in the blanks: "So God created man _____, in the

_____ of God he created him."

From this passage, how do we know that, from God's perspective, people and animals are not the same?

From these passages and other information we have in the Bible, we learn that people are far more than what the secular world recognizes. And it doesn't really matter what people think about humanity, anyway. What does God think? That's what matters. He's the creator. He made us. He knows more about us than we could ever know about ourselves. What does God say about humanity?

What does God say about you?

You were conceived, designed and created by God.

That is pretty obvious by looking at the passages above. But I want you to read and ponder another passage—Psalm 139:14-16. Look those verses up and in the space below, write down everything you see in these verses about the way the Psalmist says we were created.

Wow! That's a little different from the secular views we cited, isn't it? The Psalmist describes the wonderful design and intricate construction of every human being, even though he only scratches the surface. But he doesn't take credit for how amazing he has been made. He gives all credit to God, the mastermind, designer, creator and sustainer of every human being.

We are incredible living beings. But it all goes back to God. We are who we are because he made us to be this way.

You were conceived, designed and created by God. Consider a couple of implications of this truth...

You are NOT an accident.

You are NOT a temporary speck in a sterile mechanical world.

You ARE the crowning production of the greatest mind in the universe!

There is another obvious and very important implication that flows from all of this. If you are not just an accident, not a temporary irrelevant speck, but the crown of creation, then...

You were made for a purpose!

That matters! God made you on purpose and for a purpose! That means something!

You bear the **image** of **God.**

In the creation account of Genesis, we learn that people were created in God's image. We talked about it a little bit in the last chapter, and a lot has been said and books have been written on this subject. But let me simplify it for you.

Remember, this is something that sets people apart from animals. No animal was created in God's image, that is only said of humans. *You have characteristics and features that only humans share with God.*

In essence, the image of God in us is our spiritual capacity to relate to God and others who are created in his image, on a spiritual level.

Animals are capable of feelings and relationships, but not on a spiritual level. An animal never considers the meaning of life, why they exist, or have spiritual capacity to know about and communicate with God.

That's something only we can do. That's a capacity that God shared with us. We are the only creatures on earth that are able to relate to God and bring this unique kind of pleasure to him in a loving reciprocal relationship.

And that helps us to understand why we were created. We were created for just that, to bring joy to God in a unique way, by responding to him, loving him, communicating with him, knowing him. That's why you were created.

You can only enjoy true and lasting fulfillment in life when that purpose is satisfied.

You have an **eternal** future.

Look at Genesis 2:7. What did God do after he formed the first man from the dust of the ground?

The term here in the original Hebrew text is "khayee nephesh," or "living soul." Adam was not given a soul, he *became* a living soul when God breathed his life into Adam. Nothing like this is said in the creation account of animals. This was the life of God breathed into people and it speaks of the eternal nature of our existence.

Solomon wrote this in Ecclesiastes 3:11, "[God] has put eternity into man's heart."

You were not only created for this life, but we were created for more than just this.

C.S. Lewis was a Christian philosopher of a generation ago, and the most prolific author of the twentieth century. I love his observation in this regard.

"Creatures are not born with desires unless satisfaction for those desires exists. A baby feels hunger: well, there is such a thing as food. A duckling wants to swim: well, there is such a thing as water. Men feel sexual desire: well, there is such a thing as sex. If I find in myself a desire which no experience in this world can satisfy, the most probable explanation is that I was made for another world." – C. S. Lewis, Mere Christianity

You were created for more than this temporary life. You were given a soul that will exist in some capacity forever. God made you to be with him. He wants you to live forever with him and his family and to enjoy all that he has for you forever.

You have an eternal future!

You have a spiritual **purpose.**

You were not created for yourself. God created you for him, and not the other way around. So many people think that God should be here for them, and when he does not come to their rescue or do their bidding to their liking, they start crying, "Where is God?" As though God is in existence for *their* benefit.

We have it backwards. It's the other way around. We are here for God. Until we understand this, nothing in life will make sense. But once we get this settled, everything else starts to fall into place.

Think about it for a minute. Why would God create a world?

Why would he?

Of course, he made the world for himself... so that he could enjoy it. God created everything for his own pleasure and enjoyment.

Why would he create you? For the same reason, but with a spiritual capacity to uniquely enjoy a relationship with him, and thereby be able to fulfill a purpose far beyond anything else created.

In our home, we have two family dogs. They are cute and friendly and we love them. We've had them in our family now for quite a few years, and they bring us a lot of joy. And that's why we brought them into our home. We have Buster and Ecko for our own enjoyment and not the other way around. Because they are good dogs, friendly and playful, and they do not challenge our authority, or threaten our guests, life is good for them. They get all that they need to eat, a nice house to live in, lots of attention and affection. We care for their well-being, and they have the run of the house and yard. It's a dog's life for Buster and Ecko and they take advantage of it. But if they become a major problem and no longer contribute to our enjoyment, that would change. If they started making messes on the floor, chewing up our shoes, clothes and furniture, growling and threatening our friends or even us, they would soon be history. Because they are in our home for our enjoyment, and if that stops and they no longer serve their purpose, we would not keep them.

I know people are not dogs, but neither is God, human. While we may be far above animals in our purpose, God is even further above us in that analogy. And just as Buster and Ecko are in our home for our benefit and not the other way around, we are alive for God's benefit, and not the other way around.

We can never understand life as long as we think of God as a personal genie, a big body guard or magical tooth fairy. Many people think of God that way. But it's not who he is. He is not in existence for us; we are in existence for him! We were created by God and for God. Without this understanding, life is confusing and chaotic. But once we get that settled, everything else can begin to make sense.

He made you for **him**

When it comes to people, God created us for him to enjoy in a very special way.

The rest of creation, while made by God and for his pleasure, is not capable of interacting with him in a reciprocal loving relationship. Nothing else in creation even has an awareness that God exists. Even the most intelligent animals do not have a spiritual capacity to commune and interact with God.

But you and I can. We were created after God's image, with a living soul. It's this spiritual dimension to our existence that sets us apart in God's universe, allowing us to bring joy to him in a personal way that nothing else in the universe can.

God made you for him, so that he could enjoy a relationship with you. You were created for God's pleasure. Start there. Rather than thinking about what you want from God, ask what God wants from you.

CHAPTER 4

What's Your Problem?

I f we were created by a loving God to live forever in a relationship with Him, why are we in the mess we are in?

This is a big question and it's important to get the answer right. You can't solve a problem that isn't identified.

My grandmother died of breast cancer before I was born. I remember my mom telling us kids how she knew something was wrong and had gone to her family physician about it a couple of times. But at least twice, the doctor told her not to worry, that she simply had mastitis, and that it wasn't serious. But because he had the diagnosis wrong, the prognosis ended up being fatal.

A physician cannot correctly treat a disease that he has not accurately diagnosed.

When it comes to the problems of humanity, we have to accurately identify the root cause. Otherwise, we'll just keep treating symptoms (as we have been) and going around in circles while the world, and our personal lives, spin out of control.

There Definitely IS a Problem

A brief perusing on any internet news site makes it clear that we have some serious problems. Incidents of terrorism has become common. (Though terrorism isn't really new. Powerful despots throughout history have controlled entire continents with their brand of terrorism.)

Major acts of attempted genocide have occurred in every decade of modern history...and certainly even more so before the modern era.

Inner-city gang violence is beyond "out of control." In some cities, it is safer for an urban kid to enlist in the army and be shipped off to a hot zone, than it is for him to walk around his own neighborhood.

Racial division and even animosity is everywhere, and in every country.

Children are abused at alarming rates. Do some quick online research and look at your own town to see how many convicted sexual predators live within walking distance of your house. Google "children forced into prostitution" and see how hideous the problem is everywhere in the world.

There are more slaves today than at any other time in history. Human trafficking is one of the world's largest and most profitable businesses in the world. Adults and children are being forced into manual labor and sexual slavery every day, and many internationals are enslaved in our own country, doing manual labor or engaging in prostitution against their will.

What people do to other people is unbelievable. Murders, beatings, screaming and yelling. It's in every country, every region, every city, town and village, and some of it in every home.

You see, we don't have to look very far to find the problem. We can see it among our friends, in our own families, and when we are completely honest, within our own hearts.

The Problem is Sin

You may not be guilty of genocide, human trafficking, murder, or child abuse, but you are guilty of sin. We lie, we gossip, we argue and manipulate. We are selfish, full of pride, ungrateful, disobedient to God and often do not care or even think about what he wants from us.

Our problem: SIN.

I know it's not something that people talk about anymore. It's an archaic word and concept in a culture that would rather ignore God or at the very least, only talk about his kindness and compassion.

God is full of kindness and compassion. But he is a lot more. Because he is a good God, he also hates sin.

As we saw in the first chapter, God's goodness is not only wrapped up in his graciousness and love. He is also good because he is holy, righteous and just. If he were not also those things, he would not be good.

He is holy, meaning he is perfect. There is no flaw in him. He defines what is good and right and everything that is holy flows from him. His holiness is an essential part of his goodness.

He is also righteous, meaning that everything that he does is right. He never has done wrong, never will do wrong, and cannot do wrong. He is the epitome of all that is right, everything that comes from him is right, and all that is right flows from him.

And he is just. By God's justice, we mean that he applies his standard of righteousness to his creation. He rightly expects righteousness from those he created in his image; and being just, he demands that when his righteousness is violated, that violation must be penalized and made right.

We discussed these attributes in the first chapter, but it's important to understand this about God as we are talking about our sin problem. Because sin is a repudiation of those attributes. It's a rejection of his holiness, a violation of his righteousness, and a defiance of his justice.

We are all **infected**

And while none of us are eager to admit it, we are all guilty. The Apostle Paul said in Romans 3:23, "For everyone has sinned; we all fall short of God's glorious standard" (NLT). Jesus' best friend, John the Apostle, said this, "If we claim to be without sin, we deceive ourselves and the truth is not in us" (NLT). A common metaphor for sin in the Bible is that of disease (i.e. Mark 2:17, Revelation 3:18) and it has infected all of us.

This is not just a problem for humanity. This is my problem. And it's your problem.

To get an understanding of sin's source and its effect on humanity, I'd like you to open your Bible to Genesis 3, and in a little bit, I'm going to have you read the chapter and answer some questions about the story in it.

We are all affected

None of us are insulated from the results of sin. Our families are broken, our workplaces are contentious, our bodies are diseased and our nations are at war. People are disillusioned, depressed, and demoralized.

And the worst? We are all dying. When the first man sinned in Genesis 3, God said, "...to dust you shall return" (Genesis 3:19). Paul explained this in his letter to the Romans, "For the wages of sin is death" (Romans 6:23).

Because God is our life-giving force, and because sin is a rejection of God, the natural consequence of our rebellion against him is separation from our only life-giving source and his spiritual life. When we die physically, we will also be spiritually separated from God forever.

How it came to be

Before Genesis 3, we learned that God created everything and it was all very good. He took great pleasure in his creation. He created the first man and woman after his own image, and he breathed his own life into them as eternal souls. Everything was good. But that was about to change.

Because people were created to uniquely bring joy to God with a loving reciprocal relationship, they were also given something that nothing else in creation was given, an ability to choose to obey or disobey God.

Animals have never had a free will. They live by instinct, and essentially, nothing that an animal does is evil or sinful. They are simply acting on their instincts for self-preservation. They cannot respond to God because they are not even aware of God.

But Adam was different. He was created to know God and love God. If Adam had not been given a free will, that would not have been possible.

In order for there to be a reciprocal loving relationship, both parties have to choose it. Love, by virtue of its meaning, demands the ability to choose. God loves us, but he does not force his love on us. To force love is to commit assault, which he will not do. He loves us, he encourages our response, he woos us, he pursues us, he urges us, but he does not force us. He allows us to decide.

Could you imagine a parent demanding affection from a child and threatening punishment if they did not give it? I think of my kids when they were little. I loved nothing more than to receive their hugs and hear them say, "I love you, Daddy!" Had I demanded it, threatening, "Give me a hug right now or you're getting a spanking!" How meaningful would that affection be?

In order for God to enjoy a loving relationship with us, he gave us the ability to choose. That's why people are referred to as "moral agents." We are able to choose good or evil, obedience to God or disobedience, love or rebellion. We can love him and serve him as our God, or we can reject him and attempt to set ourselves up as our own gods (living for ourselves and for our own pleasure, rather than his).

He will not force us to follow him, obey him, or love him. He wants a genuine relationship with us. He offers himself to us, but we must choose to respond.

Before Genesis 3, God had created the world and placed Adam and Eve in it. He created them to enjoy fellowship with them, and he gave them a free will so that the relationship would be two-sided. The risk was there for them to use that free will to turn away from him, but his desire for a love relationship with us made the risk worth it.

If you haven't already, open your Bible to Genesis 3 and read the whole chapter and answer the following questions.

How does the serpent plant a seed of doubt in Eve's mind about God's command?

What false promises does the serpent make to Eve, if she were to disobey God?

What was Eve's first mistake? Track the process of this sin to the place that Adam also partakes.

What kind of fruit was this?

What did Adam and Eve do after they sinned?

How did they respond to God when he confronted them with their sin?

Why were they banished from the Garden of Eden?

What is the ultimate consequence of sin (v. 19)?

Do you find a promise for the solution to sin anywhere in this passage?

This was the first sin, not only in the Bible, but in history. Before this, everything was beautiful and good. After this, the problems began. And all the evil we see in the world today was evident in Genesis almost immediately after sin entered the picture. In the very next chapter, one of Adam and Eve's sons murders the other son. The infection and horrible effects of sin are readily apparent as soon as it began.

The word sin is used hundreds of times in our English Bibles. But the English word comes from several Hebrew (Old Testament) and Greek (New Testament) words. The most common meaning is, "missing the mark."

When you look again at Romans 3:23, "For everyone has sinned; we all fall short of God's glorious standard" (NLT), it makes sense. We've all fallen short of God's standard. We've all missed the mark.

We tend to excuse ourselves because we all know of someone else who is worse than we are. And we say things like, "I haven't murdered any-body." As though God is going to say, "I'm so proud of you! What a high standard you have set for yourself."

Maybe you haven't murdered anybody (or maybe you have), but you are a sinner and are way off the mark, way below God's standard.

Think of it this way. If we had a jumping contest over Lake Michigan, some of us would get further than others. You might out-jump me, but who cares? None of us are going to be even close! None of us are going to make it. None of us are going to win.

So, this comparing ourselves to people worse than we are is foolish. God sees us as having a jumping contest over Lake Michigan and unless he intervenes and gets us across, none of us are going to make it. Without his intervention, there are no winners. We are all going to drown!

What is sin?

Starting with the story of Adam and Eve, whenever sin is mentioned in the Bible, it was and is always people disobeying or ignoring God, doing what they want to do instead of what God wanted them to do. It might be defiance, shaking one's fist at God. Or it might be simply disregarding God, ignoring what he wants or not caring what he thinks. Either way, it leads to choices we make in conflict with God's instructions.

Remember the false promise the serpent made to Eve? He told her that if she disobeyed God, she would become "like God."

That's what we believe when we sin. We ignore the one true God by trying to arrange life around us, the way we want it, doing what we want, setting ourselves up as our own little gods. We would probably not openly say that we want to be gods. But that's what we are believing when we ignore the real God, and do as we please instead of what pleases him.

So, sin is...

– Doing what I want to do instead of what God wants me to do
– Rejecting my purpose; the reason I was created
– Setting myself up as my own god in my own world

Result

Guess what? It doesn't work.

Sin can be fun for a while. But in the end, it runs its course and leads to defeat, emptiness and despair.

Sin is the great divider. It divides us from God and from each other. The reason we have war, divorce, road rage, family feuds, office politics and animosity that people have against each other is because of sin. It cuts us off from the one who created us for relationship, and because of that, it also divides us from one another.

That's why Satan is called, "The Divider." Did you know that is the meaning of "devil"? If you know any Spanish, you know, "el diablo" (the devil) means, "the divider." That's also true of the Greek word for devil that Biblical authors used. The devil is the divider. By luring us into sin, he has divided us from God.

Here's why. By its very nature, sin separates us from God. When we say "no" to God, we reject him and leave his presence. We can't live long that way. We were created to be dependent on God. He is our life-giving source, and the only source for life. By cutting ourselves off from God, we cut ourselves off from life.

Look up Isaiah 59:1-2 and write out these verses below.

1 – Is God unable to help us?

2 – Why are we unable to get help from God?

3 – What separates us from him?

4 – Why would that be?

I read a story several years ago about a couple of young teenagers who ran away from home. Their parents were not in favor of their relationship because of their age, and so both of them no longer wanted their parents telling them what to do. They snuck out of their bedrooms one night, met up at a bus station, and took a bus to New York City. It ended tragically. A couple of men spotted the kids and intuitively knew they were runaways. They pretended to befriend them, but quickly ditched the boy and took the girl to a vacant apartment where they bound her and repeatedly raped her over the course of several days. They eventually abandoned her and though she lived through the horrible ordeal, her scars will remain with her for the rest of her life.

Retelling the story later, she said, *"When I was tied up in that apartment, every time I heard footsteps coming up the stairs and the door beginning to open, I'd cry out to my dad for help. But he wasn't there. I'd left him. I'd run away from home."*

Think about it. That girl's father had not stopped loving his little girl. He was desperately looking for her. If anything, his love for her was intensified when he learned she had run away. He was doing everything he could to bring her back.

But was she enjoying her father's love? No. She had rejected it. And she had left his protection.

Please don't misunderstand my reason for telling the story. I'm not blaming this poor girl for the horrible atrocities against her. The perpetrators were responsible and will answer to God for what they did.

But how that girl described her situation is much like the human condition.

I hear people saying, "Where is God? Why all these problems? You say he loves me…but I sure don't feel that love!" And while full answers will not be immediately revealed to us about specific difficult situations that we face, the short answers to these questions are related to that girl's retelling of her story.

We've left God. We walked away from him with our sin. We've run away from his protection. It's not that he doesn't love us. If anything, his love has intensified. And we'll see in the following chapters that he has done everything necessary to restore us to himself. But we're in the trouble we are in because we've run away from God. We've sinned. We're all guilty. And we're all in trouble because of it.

The ultimate result of sin

Sin separates us from God. It's our rebellion that has a natural consequence. When you rebel against someone, you separate yourself from that person.

When it comes to our spiritual lives, it cuts us off from where we get life from. Remember, we are not fully autonomous or completely independent creatures. We depend on God for life. Being cut off from him means death. And our sin has cut us off from God, our life-giving source.

And that's what the Scriptures teach.

Read Romans 3:23. What is a wage?

What is the wage of sin?

But this death is more than physical death. The Bible speaks of spiritual death, which is an eternal separation from God.

Read Hebrews 9:27. What comes after death for all of us?

Read Daniel 12:2. What are the eternal and final two conditions people will find themselves in after death?

Read Revelation 20:14-15. This takes place after God's final judgement. Where does this text say the final destiny of "death and hell" is?

How could God actually send people to hell? How could he be a loving God and condemn people to such a place?

The answer is found in that question. It's because of his love. He loved us enough to give us the opportunity to love him back. With that gift of freedom, came the very real possibility that we would use it to reject him, bringing the natural consequences of our sin upon us. Condemnation is the end result of God letting us go our own way without him. Having been created in his image with an eternal soul, we will exist forever somewhere. By choosing to reject him, we choose to exist forever without him. God loves us enough to respect our free will. He will not force himself upon us.

Hell is, essentially, God allowing us to go our own way.

This isn't a pleasant subject to talk about. I'd rather just say, "Don't worry about hell. I don't believe in it." But here's the problem, Jesus believed in hell. He spent much of his time on earth warning people of the reality of hell. Not because he was angry and mean-spirited. But because he loves people and he does not want them to go there.

It is something we have to talk about

Cancer is not a pleasant subject either. But I wish my Grandma's physician would have made the correct diagnosis and told her she had cancer. If he had, she could have been treated, and I might have known her. But the unpleasant reality of cancer was not correctly diagnosed. She was told not to worry, and it killed her.

Sin is not a pleasant subject and hell is even less pleasant. But Jesus loved us enough to tell us the truth. And I love you enough to pass that truth on to you.

Because of our sin, we are in a critical situation. We are in desperate need of the help that only God can give. And we need it now.

Thank God for Jesus.

CHAPTER 5

Who Is Jesus?

The timing is certainly right for this chapter. The subject matter of the last chapter left things pretty bleak. We learned that the world is in a mess, people are dying and cut off from God. And then we even learned that hell is real.

How about a happy chapter?

Well, this one is as good as it could get. In the next two chapters, we'll learn that as bad as everything is, with sin, death, condemnation and hell, that there is a resolution.

You see, just like everything else, the sin thing didn't take God by surprise. Remember that in chapter two? God isn't ever surprised. He never says, "Uh-oh." He knew this would happen. And from the very beginning of the problem, he had devised a plan so that we could be restored to our original purpose and be reconciled.

That's where Jesus comes in.

He is the Messiah

Remember how we were first introduced to our sin problem in Genesis 3? We studied that passage briefly in the last chapter. You may want to look back and refresh your memory of the story.

After the serpent convinced Eve that she could be a god by eating the forbidden fruit, and then Eve convinced Adam to eat it as well, everything changed. Sin became a part of the human condition and it was passed on to every person who has lived since. And from the very beginning, it affected people's relationship with God. Do you remember how after they sinned, Adam and Eve hid themselves from God? And we learned that that's what sin does, it cuts us off from God.

But do you also remember how God confronted them? He knew what they had done, but they still tried to deny it, and then excuse it, and then blame each other. But God didn't let it go.

What's interesting is, in that very passage, God confronted Adam and Eve and then also the serpent, who Satan employed to divide people from God. The Lord spoke to the evil one, saying,

> *"I will put enmity between you and the woman, and between your offspring and her offspring; he shall bruise your head, and you shall bruise his heel" (Genesis 3:15).*

This was the first promise of a 'coming one', the offspring of the woman, someone who would be a man, who would bruise the head of Satan while bruising his own heel. Think of the word picture.

The film, *The Passion of the Christ,* illustrated it well in the Garden scene. A serpent slithered to Jesus, who was kneeling in prayer, in an apparent attempt to tempt Jesus to reject his impending sacrifice. Jesus stood and stomped on the head of the serpent, bruising his own heel while crushing the serpent's head.

That promise of a coming one who would defeat the devil, was first alluded to when sin entered humanity and God promised a Messiah who would bruise his heel while crushing the head of Satan.

And there were many more promises. Over time, the Jewish Scriptures began to fill with imagery and prophecies of a coming Messiah who would be their deliverer. To the family of Abraham, God promised a descendent who would bring great blessing to every nation (Genesis 12:1-3).

He is the Lamb of God

Many years later, after Abraham's family had migrated to Egypt and there grew into a nation of people, they were enslaved by Pharaoh. You are probably familiar with what happened, even if just through Hollywood portrayals of the story. God called Moses to deliver Israel from slavery. Pharaoh refused to free Israel so God brought a series of ten plagues on Egypt, in order to convince Pharaoh to release them. But Pharaoh wouldn't budge. Not until the last plague.

But contained in that last plague was also a promise of spiritual deliverance for not just Israel, but all people. The final and most painful plague was the death of all firstborn sons in every family, including Pharaoh's. Pharaoh was warned and had opportunity to change his mind, but his heart was hard and he would not yield.

So, God gave instructions to the Israelites for each family to slaughter a lamb. Remember, this was a time and culture when the daily killing of animals was commonplace. It might sound cruel and inhumane to us, even while downing a hamburger, but for them, this was something that they did every day just to survive.

The strange part came next. God told the Israelites that the lamb they were to sacrifice must be perfect and without any flaws. After killing it, they were to collect all the blood from the lamb, and then paint the doorposts of their houses with that blood.

If you are familiar with the Passover story, that may not sound so strange. But for them, and anyone who has not heard this story before, that was a really bizarre request. Still, they were expected to simply trust God and do what he said.

That night, as an angel of death went throughout Egypt, killing the firstborn in every family, the households that had the blood from their flawless sacrificed lamb painted over their door posts were saved. And because they trusted God and applied the blood to their homes, that night they were released from slavery and they left Egypt as God's people.

As bizarre a request as it was, there was a picture in this that ancient people would not have missed. The blood of any animal or man was symbolic of the life of that creature. The application of the blood of the lamb to their doorposts symbolized the lamb dying in their place. They would have understood that. They probably did not grasp its full significance, but they understood the sacrificial lamb as being a substitute for them. Because the lamb died, no one in their home did.

From that time forward, the coming one that was first promised in Genesis 3 would be referred to as a lamb. The Passover became an annual feast to symbolize the coming Messiah who would deliver his people.

A short time after this, God gave to Moses what became known to them as The Law. You're familiar with the Ten Commandments. The Ten Commandments introduced and were part of this Law, which included lots of ceremonies and practices they were to keep to identify them as the Chosen People of God. This Law was filled with pictures and references to this coming one who would deliver them from spiritual bondage. Sacrificial lambs were used to symbolize a substitutionary death, that the coming Messiah would die so that they would not have to.

Throughout Israel's history, God then sent prophets to foretell to his people how a Messiah (meaning "Anointed One," "Deliverer" or "Savior") was coming and this Messiah would deliver them. Some of these prophesies pictured the Messiah as a triumphant ruler. Others pictured him as one who would suffer and die a vicarious death (like the substitutionary sacrificial lamb).

To see an example of this, read Isaiah 53:4-7 and answer the questions.

What was this person pierced and crushed for?

Whose transgressions? Whose iniquities?

How are we described in v. 6?

How does that description fit with what we talked about in the last chapter?

What does the Lord lay on this person?

What kind of animal is he compared to?

The entire Hebrew worship system was based on the sacrifice of a lamb and the hope of a coming Messiah. Everyone in Israel participated in sacrifices and everyone was looking for the promised Messiah to come.

Understanding the significance of a substitutionary lamb to their concept of forgiveness, and that the Israelites were looking for a coming Messiah, read the words of John the Baptist, as he was pointing to Jesus, in John 1:29.

What did John mean by this?

What would those he was talking to have understood him to mean?

How do you think that would have affected them?

Many years later, one of Jesus' closest friends wrote 1 Peter 1:18-19. Look it up.

What were they ransomed from?

What were they ransomed with?

Why the reference to the "lamb without spot" and why would that have been a big deal to the readers?

Before we can really understand who Jesus was and who the earliest Christians believed him to be, we have to understand the sacrificial system of the Jews and what they believed about the Messiah. The sacrificing of lambs never really did take people's sins away, it was all symbolism of what the coming Messiah would do in order to provide for our forgiveness.

Read Hebrews 10:4.

What is impossible?

Can you think of why that would be impossible?

So then why would God have instructed Israel to make those animal sacrifices?

Read v. 10. How are we actually cleansed of our sin ("sanctified" means cleansed)?

Jesus came into this world as the promised Messiah to be sacrificed or punished as our substitute. Jesus came to be the fulfillment of Isaiah 53:7. He came to take our sins on himself and die a vicarious death.

Why was it necessary for him to do that? Well, it wasn't. He didn't have to. He could have just let us remain alienated from him. But if we were to be forgiven, our sin needed to be atoned for.

That's one of the reasons why the first couple of lessons were so important. We have to understand the nature of God and the magnitude of our sin problem. God is a good God, not only because he is loving and compassionate, but also because he is holy, righteous, and just. Being a holy and just God, he must judge sin. There must be a penalty, or God would not be just. He cannot simply "put up" with our sin or he would not be holy. Because he is a good God, he demands that his justice be satisfied.

But because he is a loving God, he made the unbelievable sacrifice of becoming our substitute and taking our condemnation himself.

In order to do that, God needed to become a man. He had to be one of us to take our place. But in order to be our substitute, he also needed to be more than just a man. He needed to be perfect. And in order to satisfy the eternal nature of our penalty, he needed to be divine and immortal himself, the Son of God.

He is the Son of God

From the very beginning when Jesus first came into the world, it was obvious that he was a very special person.

For starters, there was no human father. I know it's hard to believe, but it's true. The Scriptures clearly state that when Mary, Jesus' mom, gave birth to him, she had never been with a man, sexually. She was a virgin. She knew it, and Joseph her husband knew it. You'll have to read Matthew chapter 1 and Luke 1 and 2 to get the whole story, and it's a fascinating read. But it's not just a story. It's what happened.

Jesus being born of a virgin should not have been a surprise. The prophets had said that he would be the Son of God, meaning the miraculous offspring of God. And Isaiah had prophesied hundreds of years before this that the Messiah would be born of a virgin, being conceived by God. Look up Isaiah 7:14.

What is the sign the Lord will give?

What will his name be?

The Hebrew word, Immanuel, means, "God with us." In other words, Isaiah was saying that the special sign of the coming Messiah would be that a virgin will give birth to this son, and we will then know that God is in our presence, in the person of this man.

Some have said that the Hebrew word for virgin can in some cases also just mean, "young woman." But there's a problem with that interpretation. Do you see it? It's pretty obvious. There were thousands of young women in Israel conceiving every day! How would that be a sign? No, the primary meaning of that word is virgin and that's the whole point of this prophesy. It would be a miracle, and it was.

So, Isaiah prophesied that the Messiah would be born of a virgin and that he would be the offspring of God himself. And in fact, he would be God!

When we say, "Son of God," we are talking in a very specific sense, that Jesus was God, he was and is divine. Isaiah qualified this a couple of chapters later. Look at Isaiah 9:6.

Where in this verse does Isaiah make it clear that this child will be God himself?

So, Jesus is the Son of God. He claimed to be. His closest friends and disciples believed he was, and his enemies had him crucified because he said that he was.

In Matthew 16:16, who do Jesus' close friend and disciples say that Jesus is?

In John 11:27, who does Jesus' friend, Mary of Bethany, say that Jesus is?

Read Luke 22:70. What does the High Priest ask Jesus?

How does Jesus answer?

Read John 19:7. Why did the Jewish leaders insist that Jesus must die?

So, Jesus is more than just a man, he is God. He came into this world as the Messiah, to deliver us from our condition of sin, and rescue us from sin's results. He was 100% man, with human emotions, limitations, and struggles. He is able to fully identify with us. He knows about human suffering, loneliness, discouragement and rejection. But he was more than just a man. He is God's Son, God in the flesh.

This is another one of those things that we are not going to completely grasp. But it is something we can believe. He was and is fully man and fully God. Human and divine in a merging of natures that is beyond our understanding. But what a wonderful thing for us! We have a God who knows all that we go through, who stooped to our level and even more than that, humbled himself to the place of death by crucifixion.

Wow! What a man! What a God!

He is the Savior

He did all that so that we could be saved.

Actually, the very meaning of his name is, "Savior." That's what the name Jesus means in Aramaic (the spoken form of Hebrew in Palestine when Jesus was born). His name is literally – "Jehovah (God) Saves."

When his coming was announced to Mary, she was told his name will be Jesus, because "he will save his people from their sins" (Matthew 1:21).

When his birth was announced to the shepherds, they were told, "The Messiah, the Savior had been born" (Luke 2:11).

Read John 3:17. What did Jesus say he came into the world to do?

Read Luke 19:10. Why does he say in this verse that he came?

Read 1 Timothy 1:15. Why did Paul say Jesus came?

But what does that mean? What does it mean that Jesus is the Savior. If he came to save the lost, and we are the lost (we've already established that), then how did he do that? What did he do to save us?

We've already alluded to that when we learned that Jesus came as the lamb of God to be sacrificed for us. Let's look at Romans 5:6-11 and answer the questions.

Who did Christ die for (the word, "Christ" means "Messiah")?

How did God show his love for us?

Because of his blood (meaning "put to death"), what are we saved from?

What does it mean to be "reconciled"?

He died to save us

How he did this is hard for us to fathom. It is incredible that God would go to the lengths he did for our reconciliation. He literally entered the human race and became a person, like us. He assumed the limitations of humanity, and fulfilled all that God expected of us by living an absolutely perfect life. He lived a sinless and perfect life on our behalf. *He was everything that we were supposed to be.*

And then, he also took upon himself our sin and guilt and experienced condemnation for us. Jesus did not deserve any kind of punishment; he was perfect. We are the guilty ones who brought condemnation on ourselves with our sin. But Jesus was unjustly condemned and tortured to death by crucifixion, assuming the penalty we deserve.

Something happened to Jesus as he was dying that is beyond our understanding. While he was hanging on the cross as an innocent man, he absorbed all of our guilt from everything we have ever done in offense to God. And then he experienced the horrible spiritual ordeal of being separated from the Father. He was cut off from his heavenly Father, and he died, condemned, naked, alone, with a burst of indescribable spiritual and physical pain. He was condemned, so that we could be saved.

He rose again to deliver us

Look back again at Romans 5 and notice in verse 10, the words, "...shall we be saved by his life." That's a reference to Jesus' resurrection. And that's a really important part of what Jesus did to save us.

According to the Bible, Jesus died on our behalf, or as our substitute. But he did not stay dead. Because he is also God, he was able to defeat death and he rose again, conquering sin's penalty. Through his resurrection, he made a new resurrected spiritual life available to us. Here's what

Paul said in Romans 4:25:

> *"He was handed over to die because of our sins, and he was raised to life to make us right with God" (Romans 4:25 NLT).*

Here's what Peter said:

> *"Christ suffered for our sins once for all time. He never sinned, but he died for sinners to bring you safely home to God. He suffered physical death, but he was raised to life in the Spirit" (1 Peter 3:18 NLT).*

The Bible describes it this way: It was our sin that died with Jesus and was buried in his grave. It was our resurrection that Jesus accomplished when he came back from the dead. We can now receive Jesus' new and resurrected life in the same way he received our sin on the cross. His death was vicarious and his resurrection is also vicarious.

Read Galatians 2:20. What does Paul mean by, "I have been crucified with Christ?"

What then does he say about the life he has?

How is that related to Jesus' resurrection?

Read Romans 6:4. How does baptism (baptism was an immersion in Bible times) picture a Christian's connection with Jesus's death and resurrection?

Explain, "Just as Christ was raised from the dead through the glory of the Father, we too may live a new life" (Romans 6:4).

Just as his death was vicarious—for us, his resurrection is also vicarious—on our behalf. When we put our faith in him, we are spiritually resurrected because of his resurrection, and we receive Jesus' resurrected life in us.

This is very important to understand. Everything about Jesus comes down to his resurrection. Jesus' resurrection from the dead was the greatest event in history. While his death on our behalf was necessary for our forgiveness, we are released from sin's penalty (death) because of Jesus' resurrection.

Referring to his promised resurrection from the dead, Jesus said, "Because I live, you will live also" (John 14:19). So, we can have a new resurrected spiritual life because of Jesus' resurrection from the dead.

In 1 Corinthians 15, Paul defined the gospel (the message of Christians, meaning "good news") as Jesus dying for us and rising from the dead. He went on to say that if Jesus had not risen from the dead, we would not be able to live again, we would be miserable, and our faith would be empty.

But because he rose from the dead, we can be saved from death's grip, and it has no power over us any longer.

That's what he came here for. He came to die and be resurrected so that we could be saved.

CHAPTER 6

Get a New Life

Don't be offended by this chapter title, but as we learned, because of sin, we have lost the life God has for us. This chapter is about how we can get it back.

To review, remember who God is and remember who we are. He is the creator; we are his creation. We were formed as incredible beings to be his crown of creation. We were made after his image and are capable of reflecting many of his attributes, including moral goodness.

But in order to be truly good, we have to be able to make the choice to do good. If we had no choice, we would simply be programmed biological robots and our supposed love for him would be coerced and not a genuine choice.

With that ability to choose, all of us have turned away from God and have sinned.

That's what sin is, turning away from God. Being a good God, he loves us and does not want to see us go. But also, being good, he is holy and just. He cannot sanction our rebellion. He respects our decision to abandon him and he allows us to go our own way, bringing the natural consequences of sin on ourselves, separation from him and its resulting condemnation, forever.

But being a good God, he still loves us and desires for us to be reconciled to him, so he devised a plan for us to be returned in a renewed relationship with him. That's what the last chapter was about, how God entered the human race in order to save us.

Jesus was the Messiah who was promised as soon as sin came into the picture. He was prophesied as the Passover lamb. The prophets foretold that he would become our substitute, that he would take our condemnation and suffer and die in our place. He was both man and God, the perfect infusion of human and divine natures, putting him in the unique position to satisfy the penalty of sin and reconcile us to the Father.

He was a perfectly innocent man who had never done anything wrong. He deserved no punishment. We are the ones who have sinned. But because of his love for us, he accepted the condemnation of our sin and he died in our place so that we could be forgiven.

But then he rose again from the dead, securing new life for us with his resurrection.

It's the ONLY Way

Jesus clearly claimed that the only way for us to get back to being what we were created to be, the only way for us to be reconciled to God, is through him.

Read John 14:6. What three things does Jesus say that he is?

What does he mean by each of these things?

How many ways are there to get to heaven?

Is there any way to be reconciled to God other than through Jesus?

Read Acts 4:12 and write what this verse teaches:

I know that comes across as being exclusive. And because of this, Christians are accused of being exclusive. But bear in mind that all of the world's religions claim to have the corner on truth. The difference between Christianity and the world's religions is that *Jesus welcomes all.* You do not have to be a certain gender, race, wear accepted clothing, pay a fee or practice required rituals. There is only one way, but that one way is available to anyone.

Think of a country club. Which is more exclusive? The club that requires a high fee, maintains a dress code, and only welcomes invited guests? Or the club that advertises, "Come one, come all. There is no entrance fee. But the only way in is through the main entrance."

God devised a way for us to be brought back into fellowship with him and that way is through Jesus. We don't have the privilege of deciding what we want to believe about God or how to get to heaven. That's up to God. And the way he says to heaven is through his son, Jesus. We can be restored to life with God and eternity in heaven if we come to God through Jesus.

So then, how do we do that? How can you know for sure that you are saved?

Believe in Jesus

One evening, after a long day of traveling, teaching, healing, and interacting with people, Jesus was relaxing at home when there was a knock at his door. It was a wealthy young man named Nicodemus. He was a Pharisee.

The Pharisees were a very religious sect that had gained power in the religious and political systems in Israel. They were legalistic, harsh and most were greedy for power and money. But they were super religious. They had to have major portions of the Torah memorized and their clothing was filled with religious imagery. They would have writings from the Torah attached to their arms and even along the sides of their eyes so that they could read and memorize Scriptures at any time. They were known to stop in the middle of the street and recite long and loud prayers. People saw them as spiritual giants.

But Jesus didn't. Because of his teaching on love and grace, they wrote him off. Yet because of his popularity, many Pharisees felt threatened by him. When he began to declare himself to be the Messiah and the Son of God, they led the charge to have him put to death.

And there stood Nicodemus that night, in all of his religious clothing and with all of his knowledge of the Law and memorized Scriptures. But there was something about Jesus and his teaching that made Nicodemus doubt the path he was on, and he wanted to learn more about what Jesus was teaching. Being a Pharisee, and not wanting other Pharisees to know that he was visiting Jesus, he quietly and in the darkness of night, went to the house where Jesus was staying.

Before the conversation even got under way, Jesus locked eyes with this young man and said, "If you are going to enter the kingdom of heaven, you must be born again."

Wow! Even with everything that Nicodemus had done and was doing, Jesus seemed to be saying, "That's not going to get you there. Your religion won't save you. You need something deeper. You need a spiritual birth. You need a new life."

Nicodemus was confused and Jesus explained himself further. And then he gave some of the most famous words in history. It was in this conversation that Jesus said:

> *"For God so loved the world, that he gave his only Son, that whoever believes in him should not perish but have eternal life" (John 3:16 ESV).*

There we have it. Everything we've talked about up until now in a nutshell. God loves you so much that he sent his son, the Messiah. If you will believe in him, you will not be condemned, but you will be given eternal life.

What? No rituals? No good works to make up for all the bad things? No church membership? That's it? Just believe?

That's what Jesus said, "Believe in me."

It's pretty important that we talk about that word, "believe." Our being saved depends on it so we better know what it means.

Our English translation doesn't tell all. This was originally written in Greek, and the Greek word for believe here is the word, "pisteuō." When we say, "believe," we mean to mentally agree with something as true. But this word is stronger than that. It is often translated, "faith," "trust," "depend on," or "commit to."

I love the story told about the great 19th century acrobat Charles Blondin. He was a famous circus showman who was known for daring high-wire tightrope acts. On three occasions, he had a wire strung across Niagara Falls and huge crowds watched as he went across doing a number of feats. All of that is true and there are pictures of him on a wire above Niagara Falls all over the internet.

But the story is told of how on one occasion he asked the crowd if they believed he could take a wheelbarrow across the falls and back. This would be difficult both because of the extra weight he'd have to push, and he would also not have a pole to help with his balance. Plus, the area surrounding the falls was filled with high winds and a constant thundering vibration. But the crowd went wild and they chanted, "We believe you can!" Then he asked, "Do you believe I can put a man in this wheelbarrow and push him across and back?" Of course, the crowd really began to cheer and shout, "Yes! We believe you can!"

Then he asked, "Who will volunteer to get into the wheelbarrow?"

The crowd went silent.

As the story goes, a little boy volunteered but his wise mother wouldn't let him do it. And that's when Blondin addressed the crowd.

"That's the difference between faith and belief. You all say that you believe in me. But only this little boy has faith in me."

That's pisteuō, the word Jesus used in John 3:16. It's getting in the wheelbarrow.

Are you ready to believe in Jesus like that? Are you ready for that kind of belief? Will you get into the wheelbarrow and trust in him to take you through life and into eternity?

Repent of Your Sin

Another word that is used a lot in the Bible regarding our salvation is the word, "repent." When we understand the meaning of *believe* properly, and understand what repent means, we can see that the two concepts are different sides of the same coin.

Let's first look up some Scripture.

Matthew 3:1-2. What was the central theme of John the Baptist's message?

Matthew 4:17. What was the theme of Jesus' preaching?

Mark 1:14-15. What needs to happen in order for us to believe the gospel (good news).

That's something important for us to know. Repentance is part of believing or trusting fully in Jesus. In order for us to depend only on him, we have to let go of whatever it is that is keeping us from doing that.

Repentance means "turning." The Greek word (metanoia) literally means to change our mind about something, but it was always used in the context of also changing actions. In other words, it's a turning around in the way we think about something, so that the natural result will be a change in behavior.

Because of our sin, we have ourselves seated on the thrones of our hearts. We view ourselves as our own bosses. 'Lord' is the term used in Scripture—we are our own lords or our own gods.

Repentance is saying, "My own way is the wrong way. I don't want my way anymore. I want God's way, now. I don't want to be in charge anymore. I want Jesus to be in charge."

Repentance is an attitude about the sin that keeps us from being able to get into the wheelbarrow. When we repent, we are able to fully trust in Jesus.

Not only was this Jesus' message, it was the message proclaimed by his disciples. In Mark 6, Jesus sent his disciples out to bring his message and the theme of their preaching was also, "Repent" (Mark 6:12). Let's look at a couple more Scriptures.

In Acts 3:19, who was the preacher?

What did he say needed to happen for their sins to be wiped away?

According to Acts 17:30, who needs to do this?

In 2 Peter 3:9, what does God not want people to do?

What is the alternative?

There are many more Scriptures that we could look at and this concept is put in other ways. Later, when we examine Romans 10, we'll see that Paul uses the common understanding in the ancient world of "lordship." Because the Jews refused to utter God's proper name, they referred to him as, "Lord" or we would say, "Master" or even, "Boss." After Jesus came, his followers referred to him as "Lord," which was a reference to his deity. In the Greco-Roman culture, a lord was whoever was in charge. So, to acknowledge Jesus as "Lord" for the early Christians, it meant that they were acknowledging both his deity and his place as master, that he is their boss. To proclaim Jesus as Lord was an expression of repentance. No longer would they be their own gods. They were proclaiming Jesus to be their God. That's what repentance is: turning from self and turning to God.

Receive the gift of salvation

After hearing about what Jesus did for us in the last chapter, we might think, "Great, Jesus took care of everything. We can now go to heaven."

True, but he leaves an important choice up to you. God is not going to grab you by the hair and drag you off to his cave. He is not going to kidnap you and hold you hostage, forcing you to be with him. He did everything necessary for your sins to be forgiven and for you to be reconciled with him. But you must respond.

Read Romans 6:23 again (we looked at it briefly in chapter 3). After it talks about the "wages of sin," what does it say salvation is?

What's the difference between a wage and a gift?

Read John 1:12. What is the gift in this verse?

According to this verse, is everyone a child of God?

Who is able to become children of God?

Look at the next verse (v. 13). When this happens, what does John call this?

Do you remember where else we heard salvation described this way?

The Bible describes what Jesus did for us as a gift, that salvation is a gift that must be received. And when we receive it, we are given new spiritual life.

Sometimes we look at a gift and admire the packaging. We see the way it is wrapped in colorful paper with an attractive bow. It looks so nice that we almost hate to open it. But that is what the gift is for. The packing is just a glimpse of the value of what lies inside.

The story of Jesus is a beautiful one. But God didn't go through all that he did so that you could just sit back and admire the beautiful story of the gospel. He sent his Son to give his life for you so that you could receive it, be forgiven, and be saved and have his new life. He is offering you that gift of salvation now, and he wants you to take it.

You do that by repenting of your sin and believing in Jesus. If you are sincerely sorry for your sin and you are ready to get into Jesus' wheelbarrow, then just tell him that, and ask him to save you. He promised that he will.

Read Romans 10:9-10. What does it mean to confess "Jesus as Lord"?

What does it mean to "believe"?

In order to be saved, what is it that we are to depend on or trust in?

If we confess Jesus as Lord (repent) and have faith in his resurrection, what does he promise?

Now jump down to verse 13. What does it say?

So, if you are ready to renounce your sin (repentance) and willing to completely depend on Jesus' death for you and his resurrection to give you new life (faith), all you have to do is ask him to save you and he promised he would.

Let's close the chapter this way. Answer these questions:

Do you understand that you are a sinner and that you have offended a righteous and holy God?

Do you believe that Jesus is God's Son and that he died for you and that he rose again from the dead?

Are you ready to repent, or renounce your rebellion against God, and receive his gift of salvation, allowing him to become the leader of your life?

If you wrote, *"yes,"* to those questions, then simply pray something like this, and sincerely mean it. (I suggest you pray it out loud for your own benefit.)

"God, I know that I have sinned against you and I am sorry. I believe that Jesus died for me and that he rose again from the dead. I am trusting in you to save me because of what Jesus did for me. Please forgive me and receive me into your family. Please take me to heaven when it is time. I ask you this in Jesus' name."

Did you pray that prayer and mean it? Look back at Romans 10:13 again.

What does God promise to those who called on his name, asking to be saved?

Did you?

Then, according to God's promise, are you saved?

If you are sincerely sorry for your sin and believing that Jesus died for you and rose again, if you called on him and asked him to save you, he promised he would. And he will never lie!

For your own keepsake, if this is something you did, sign and date below.

_____

(sign once you've prayed)

_____

(date)

CHAPTER 7

You're In The Family Now

Welcome to the family!

Some of you who are reading this just recently received Jesus and you are now a committed follower of Jesus. I'm sure that there are others of you who weren't sure where you were with God but settled it in the last chapter. Or, maybe you've been a Christian for a long time but are doing this study to learn more and to grow.

Whatever the case may be for you, if you now believe in Jesus and what he did for you to save you, and he's your master, then you are in his family.

That's what the church is. It's the family of God.

You see, the local church is a gift from God to his followers. Jesus provided his people a way to enjoy God's family before heaven. While lots of people criticize, complain about and malign the church, the church was Jesus' idea and as imperfect as it may be (it's made up of people), he expects his followers to join and participate in a Bible-teaching local church where they can learn, grow, fellowship, serve, give and help the kingdom of God accomplish its mission.

In this chapter, you will learn what God's vision is for a church, that is, what it should be. You will also learn how you can be a part of making your church all that God wants it to be.

If your church is a biblical one, it will be there for you to help you in many ways. But if you are a follower of Jesus, you will also want to be there for your church, to help God's family, your brothers and sisters in

Christ, in just as many ways.

The church has a lot to offer you. But also, as a Christian, you have a lot to offer the church. That's why Jesus established it!

How often have you heard people say something like, "I'm ok with Jesus, but I don't like organized religion." Maybe you've even said something like that in the past. But think about what that is saying. It's not organizing a thing that makes it bad. The opposite of organization is chaos. Bringing order to something, by nature, improves it. Healthy organization puts good things together in order to accomplish more good.

Sin and chaos makes things bad. Not organization.

If it were not for God's people being organized, there are a lot of good things that would not have been accomplished. The plight of women would never have been elevated. Women were viewed as property virtually everywhere around the world before the influence of the church. The church was the first place in history where women were viewed as equals on a large scale.

It was through the organized church that modern education was developed, health care systems and hospitals were founded, slavery was abolished, the civil rights movement was birthed, AIDS & deadly infectious diseases world-wide have been alleviated, and the relief of very serious starvation and poverty has been impacted in a major way.

The fight against human trafficking today is being led by organized Christian groups. One leader in the fight against international human trafficking told me that were it not for the church, virtually nothing would be happening.

When you hear someone talk down the church, just remind them that the church of Jesus Christ has been the most powerful movement for good in all of history.

Because of its power, many people have hypocritically used it for self-serving and evil purposes. But that proves the point. Their "Christianity" is counterfeit. They wouldn't be trying to counterfeit the church if there wasn't a genuine article that has been such a force for good. It only makes sense to counterfeit a genuine article. Have you ever heard of a counterfeit

$3 bill? Of course not. Only genuine articles are counterfeited.

So yes, there are hypocrites and counterfeits who have injured the reputation of the church. But it's up to us, sincere followers of Jesus, to show the world what the church *really* is. Instead of abandoning her or joining other critics, let's be the church that Jesus envisioned when he established it.

I'd like to challenge you to join forces with God's family and experience the church like you've never experienced it before.

What a Church Is

There is a lot of misunderstanding of what a church is. Some think of a location, a church building. Others think of a church as an international or national denomination. But these do not fit with the way churches were described in the Bible.

Every time the word, "church" appears in our English Bibles, the original Greek word is, "ekklesia." While our English word church is exclusively a religious term, the Greek word, ekklesia, was not. It literally means, "called-out ones" but was commonly understood as, "assembly" or "gathering."

The word has an interesting history. In the ancient Greek city-states, the community was run as a democracy. Whenever there was to be a meeting of citizens, a page would walk up and down the city streets and "call out" for the citizens to gather at the governing hall. The gathering was referred to as the "ekklesia" or the "called-out ones."

We can see why Jesus chose this word for his church. He was the first to use the term for a religious gathering of any kind. But it makes sense, because the church is made up of those who have been called out from the world to be a gathering in Jesus' name.

There are two aspects of the church. One is what we would call the universal church, or all genuine followers of Jesus around the world. The universal church cannot really assemble or organize, but it will someday. Hebrews 12:23 speaks of an assembly of all believers who will gather in heaven. In some places in the New Testament where the word church is used, it's talking about all believers.

But most of the time, the word church refers to a local church, a group of Christians who were organized with leaders in a local area and gathered together weekly for worship, prayer, teaching, baptisms and communion, and were working together to represent Jesus and proclaim the gospel in their city or area.

Metaphors of the Church

There are a number of metaphors or analogies that are used in the New Testament to describe both local churches and the universal church. These pictures of the church show us how precious the church is to God, and how important it is for followers of Christ. Based on these analogies, the church is a big deal to God, and ought to be a big deal to us.

Jesus' Family

A New Testament church is a community of Christ-followers who see themselves as family. The early believers called each other "brother" and "sister" and referred to themselves as a household of faith (Galatians 6:10). That's what the church was in the New Testament, and that's what a church should be today.

The way early Christians viewed and treated each other as being brothers and sisters, and family members had a huge impact on people who knew them in the Roman world. They had never before witnessed the kind of unconditional love, forgiveness, loyalty, commitment, and care for one another that these early Christians had for each other in the church. Especially since the Roman world was highly segregated and divided by ethnicity, language, and economic status. They couldn't believe that wealthy land owners and politicians would pray and worship together, as well as serve side-by-side with slaves. In the church, cultures, races, and classes all came together, worshipped and served together, treating each other as equals, and cared for each other as though they were blood relatives. Many were drawn to Christianity in the Roman world because these early Christians practiced what Jesus taught, *"Just as I have loved you, you should love each other. Your love for one another will prove to the world that you are my disciples"* (John 13:34-35 NLT).

Our family used to take family vacations out west when our kids were young. After hours in a vehicle together, pulling a camper in the mountains, you can imagine how easy it would have been for three very different kids to start to get on each other's nerves. And they did. But imagine our oldest jumping out at a filling station, and seeing another family's vehicle at a nearby pump, and jumping into that car, "I'm switching families. The old one is annoying me. This other one looks a lot cooler."

Yet, that's the kind of commitment a lot of church members have for their church. It's a family "for a while." But as soon as they get offended, or bored, or another cooler church launches down the road, that *family* is history.

It's not exactly what Jesus had in mind.

What are some ramifications of this, that the church is God's family?

What does it tell us about God's love for his church?

How should this affect the way we treat each other in the church?

Jesus' Body

The early Christians also referred to the church as the body of Christ, meaning it is the physical manifestation of Jesus on earth. It is through the church that Jesus does his work. It is the only way people will be able to see what Jesus is like. We are his body.

In 1 Corinthians 12:27, Paul wrote, "Now you are the body of Christ and individually members of it." Here, he emphasizes how, as individual believers, we are different, and bring different gifts and diversity to the church, to build her and serve her. We are like different body parts, but together we make up the body.

Something interesting that also comes from this passage and a similar passage in Romans 12, is the concept of church membership. I've heard some say that church membership is not in the Bible. But nothing could be further from the truth.

The word "membership" is of Christian origin, and it comes from Romans 12 and 1 Corinthians 12, where, the Apostle Paul taught the idea of individuals in a church being "members" or "body parts" of the larger body. The reason we speak of any kind of organizational membership is because of this body of Christ analogy, and how individuals in a church are members of the body of Christ.

What does the church being Jesus' body tell us about God's love for the church?

How does this speak to our responsibility to be actively involved in our church?

What does this say about our need to promote peace and unity in the church?

Based on this analogy, how would you respond to someone who says, "I'm cool with Jesus, but not the church."?

Jesus' Temple

In Ephesians 2:20-22 Paul wrote, speaking of the church, "…built on the foundation of the apostles and prophets, Christ Jesus himself being the cornerstone, in whom the whole structure, being joined together, grows into a holy temple in the Lord. In him you also are being built together into a dwelling place for God by the Spirit."

Paul was saying that the church is the place where God meets with his people and receives their corporate worship. That's not a popular view in our American individualistic culture, where the emphasis is on individuals having a relationship with God. This is certainly important, but the teaching of the Bible is that God requires his people to come together in corporate worship. In the Old Testament, this was done through the Temple. But in the New Testament, Jesus taught that our worship is to be in spirit, that it's not a place that's important, but a coming together of God's people in a corporate worship gathering, wherever that may be. Paul was teaching in Ephesians 2 (above) that the dwelling of God is not in a place, but in the presence of God's people gathered together.

In 1 Corinthians 3:16-17, Paul wrote to the church in Corinth, "Do you not know that you are God's temple and that God's Spirit dwells in you? …God's temple is holy, and you are that temple." In this passage, the "you" is plural in the original Greek, but "temple" is singular. Paul was saying, "You together make up the temple of God. God is present in your gathering and he receives your worship as you come together."

I am from Wisconsin and pastored in that state for almost twenty years. Because so many loved the outdoors and our church and town were filled with hunters and fishermen (I'm also an avid outdoorsman), I would often hear, "Pastor, I don't need to be in church to worship God. I can worship God out in the woods, in my deer stand, or on the lake with a fishing pole."

But is it true? Not according to Scripture. While I agree that everything we do is to be for God's glory and we worship God by the way we live, there is an element of worship that God requires from his people that only occurs when we come together as God's temple in the church.

This is something that virtually all Christians understood, believed, and practiced for seventeen hundred years. It was not until the American era with its emphasis on individualism when interpreters began to see the temple as an individual Christian. But this is not what Paul was teaching in 1 Corinthians 3, and certainly not in Ephesians 2. While God wants us to acknowledge his power and holiness and goodness as individuals, instructions for us to worship in Scripture were for corporate gatherings, worshipping in community. You can worship God on your own, but if you do not gather with his family regularly for corporate worship, you aren't really worshiping him on your own, either. You are ignoring his command.

So, yes, God desires a personal relationship with you as an individual. We saw that in our last chapter. But when he saved you, he saved you to be a part of his family, his kingdom, for you to be a building block in his temple. The New Testament knows nothing of 'Lone Ranger' Christianity. The New Testament teaches that being a Christian means that you have been called out of your own world, and placed into Jesus' community of believers, his church.

Jesus' Bride

The church is also called the bride of Christ. In Ephesians 5, Paul gave instructions to husbands and wives in their relationship, and in doing so, he compared their responsibilities to each other to Jesus and the church. In 2 Corinthians 11:2, Paul was referring to his ministry to the Corinthian church in influencing them toward Christ, *"I promised you as a pure bride to one husband—Christ"* (NLT).

Read Ephesians 5:22-33. To what does Paul compare the husband-wife relationship?

Who is the church compared to?

Who is Christ compared to?

How was this to affect both of their conduct?

Who seems to have the seemingly impossible job in this passage?

How is the care that Jesus has for his church described?

How should that affect our attitude toward his church, in terms of the way we talk about her?

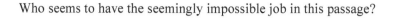

A fairly popular author in Christian leadership circles had written a se-ries of books that came across to me as unfairly critical of churches. He was trying to promote his new way of doing church, and was contrasting his views with the way many western churches operate. But his descrip-tions were very broad and general, and quite different from my experience in local churches. I stopped reading this man's books because of the atti-tude I felt he conveyed. But I was pleasantly surprised when he came out with a revised tone in later speaking engagements and made the statement, *"Don't ever ridicule the bride of Christ no matter what she may look like because sooner or later you will have to deal with the groom."*

No doubt, the church has its flaws. And not every organization that calls itself a church can rightly be described as a New Testament church. Some churches are lifeless, lack Biblical teaching, and could better be described as social clubs. I get that. And I grew up going to a church that was very boring and it did little for me.

But on the other hand, having been in local church ministry for over thirty years, the best people I have ever known, the most honest, authentic, humble and gracious people I have ever met, have been church people. When I became a committed follower of Jesus at the age of 17, my local church became my family, closer to me than my blood family. They took me in, loved me, taught me, cared for me, mentored me, and equipped me to serve God and other people. Now, these many years later, the church is still my family.

When you think of it, our own flesh and blood will only be family in eternity if they are also related to us through Jesus and thereby becoming family in the church. It's our spiritual family that we will enjoy for eternity. So, my greatest goal as a father has always been to see my biological children become "church family."

As insiders, we should always be on the lookout for needed changes, false teaching, and hypocrisy. And we should do our best to make necessary changes, out of love for Jesus, his church, and one another. But we must be on guard against that critical spirit that is so prevalent among professing Christians. Rather than tearing down the bride of Christ, we are to love and care for her, and help her to become all that Jesus has called her to be.

What a Church is For

Ever hear of 'Market Myopia'? It's a term used in marketing for the mistake that companies make when they are short-sighted and focus on their own immediate wants and preferences as opposed to seeing the big picture and understanding what the purpose of their business is.

For example, the railroad people didn't realize they were in the transportation business; they thought they were in the railroad business. Had they realized they were in the transportation business they would have invested in the airplane. The telegraph people thought they were in the telegraph business instead of the communications business. In 1886 or so, they could have bought all the telephone patents for $40,000. So obviously these people didn't know what business they were in. In recent years with the rapid changes in technology, many companies have been driven out of business for that very reason.

And I think it's a big problem for the church.

Most Christians have no idea what a church is for. So, they focus on their personal preferences, fight about silly disagreements, jockey for influence, complain, criticize one another, pout when they don't get their way, busy themselves in a flurry of empty activity. All because they don't know what they are in existence for. But when they get that figured out and everyone rallies around the mission, everything changes.

Jesus made the church's purpose pretty clear. Just before he left the earth, after spending three years teaching and training the small group who would become the leadership team of the first church, he met with them for some final words. Look at Matthew 28:18-20. These were his marching orders. This is what he was telling them the church was supposed to do:

Matthew 28:18-20

Who was Jesus talking to (v. 16)?

Do you know who the elders were in the first church?

How long do you think it was after Jesus said this, before the church was started?

A lot of people think that Jesus told the disciples to do three things. But he doesn't really. He tells them to do *one* thing, and then two others would be part of doing that one thing. Read vv. 19-20 again. What is that *one* thing he told them to do?

In the Bible, only people who committed themselves to be followers of Jesus were baptized. Why do you think this was included and an important part of the one thing that the church was supposed to do?

Why would "teaching them…" also be an important part of that one thing they were to do?

Do you see how "teaching them…" would help them to go full circle, and help them to accomplish that one thing?

This wasn't a brand-new thing for the disciples to hear. This is what Jesus had always taught them. From the day he met the first disciples he told them, "Follow me and I will make you fishers of men" (Matthew 4:19).

He always taught his followers to look outside of themselves and reach out to others.

He said, "Look unto the fields. They are white and ready for harvest" (John 4:35).

In John 10:10, he said, "I came that *they* may have life."

Notice, he did not say, "I came that *you* may have life." He said, I came that *they* may have life," because he wanted his followers to be thinking of others' need for salvation.

While he was with them he sent them out on a training mission two-by-two. And what were they to do? Proclaim the gospel. When he first spoke of the church to them, here's what he said, "The gates of hell will not hold up against it!" (Matthew 16:18).

In other words, the church was to be attacking the gates of hell—proclaiming the gospel and pulling people from the fire (as Jude put it – Jude 23).

When you think about it, everything else that we do in church, we'll be able to do even better in heaven. We'll fellowship in perfect harmony in heaven. Our worship songs will be sung directly to God in person. Our praying will also be in person. We will be learning Jesus' teaching directly from him. Everything else that churches do we will continue to do in heaven. But this one thing—making disciples—we can only do that now. That's what a church is for.

If we rally around that mission, pour ourselves into accomplishing what is dearest to the heart of Jesus, and arrange everything in the church around that goal, everything else will take care of itself. We'll worship with more sincerity. We'll fellowship with greater love and forgiveness. We'll listen to the Word more intently. We'll get along better and we'll accomplish more. Because all of those other things will be aimed at the target that Jesus gave us, disciple-making.

What a Church Does

But in order to accomplish the mission of making disciples, the church does a lot of things. This is probably why a lot of us get confused about the purpose of the church. We confuse what churches do with what a church is for. The church is for reaching lost people and then helping them grow so that they in turn can reach other lost people. But we do a number of things with the long-term goal of accomplishing that.

Read Acts 2:41-42. This tells the story of the church in its earliest days.

Who was baptized in v. 41?

How large was this church when it started?

What should that tell us about what God thinks of large churches?

What were these early Christians devoted to doing in their church?

What stands out to you about the attitude they had toward each other?

Look up Galatians 6:10. Paul tells us to be good to everyone, but especially who?

Who would that have been?

What is the significance of this?

When we look at the above verses, a few things stand out that the early church did, and any church that is patterned after the New Testament will focus on doing.

Evangelize

This word comes from the Greek word for gospel, *euongelizo*, and it means, "proclaim the gospel." The gospel message is what I shared in chapter 6, how Jesus died for us and rose again and we can be saved by trusting in Jesus. The early church actively proclaimed this. In fact, we can see in the Acts 2 account, it's how the church was born. Peter, one of the founders, proclaimed the gospel and 3,000 responded and were baptized. As we continue to read the book of Acts, we learn that the early church was consumed with the gospel and its proclamation. It's why Paul wrote to the Romans, "For I am not ashamed of the gospel, for it is the power of God for salvation to everyone who believes" (Romans 1:16).

Read 2 Timothy 4:5. What "work" did Paul tell Timothy he should do?

What would that have meant to Timothy?

Baptize

When the first Christians became believers, we learn that the apostles immediately baptized them.

Baptism for the early Christians was a way for them to publicly express their identification with Jesus' death, burial and resurrection. And as we read through the New Testament, it becomes apparent that they all did it. Every one of them got baptized shortly after they committed their lives to following Jesus. It was a kind of initiation into Christianity, their way of showing that they were serious about being with Jesus.

Read Acts 2:41. What did the people who believed, do, immediately, to show that they believed?

Read Acts 8:12. What did these people do after they believed?

Read Romans 6:3-4. What work of Jesus is symbolized with baptism?

Why then, is it a big deal for us to be baptized?

If you have received Jesus but have not been baptized, talk with the person doing this study with you or your pastor about how you can follow through on this important sacrament.

Teach

In Acts 2, we also read that the early church gathered faithfully to hear the apostles' teaching. This was a big part of the early church's gathering, and it has been ever since. Pastors are charged with the responsibility to teach God's Word so that people can know and understand what is in the Bible, and also so that they can apply it to their lives and put the things taught into practice. Any true New Testament church will teach the Bible in an accurate, compelling and practical way.

Read 2 Timothy 4:2. Timothy was a young pastor. What does Paul tell him to do here?

In what manner was he supposed to do this?

What does that tell us about how we should receive teaching and preaching of the Bible?

Worship

Communion:

On Jesus' last night with his disciples, before he was betrayed, tried, and put to death, he shared a final meal with them. In that meal, he compared his body to the bread they were eating and his blood to the wine they were drinking. He then instructed them to continue this practice in the future to remember him and his impending sacrificial death.

From the earliest days of the church, they did just that. The author of Acts also refers to the early church "breaking bread" together. While this could refer to shared meals, most commentators understand this as the early practice of communion, or remembering Jesus' sacrifice by reenacting the Lord's Supper.

Having communion together, then as now, would have been an element of corporate worship. The Lord's Supper was Jesus' final meal with his disciples before he died, when he asked them to continue to do it regularly to remember him. That's what communion is. It is a time to remember what Jesus asked us to remember.

The unleavened bread (an element in the Passover meal that Jesus referred to) represents Jesus' broken body, and the physical pain he suffered on our behalf. The drink (fermented or unfermented) represents Jesus' shed blood, his death on our behalf that provided for our forgiveness.

Communion in and of itself has no saving value. But because we are saved, we will want to remember what Jesus did for us in order that we could be saved. Some churches do this weekly, some monthly. The Bible does not specify how often we should.

Read 1 Corinthians 11:23-28. Where does Paul get these instructions?

From the words of Jesus, why does he say we should take communion?

What would an "unworthy manner" be?

So then, what does he say we should do as we take communion?

Prayer

Acts 2 also reports that the early believers gathered to pray. Jesus promised that when only a couple of us gather in his name to pray, he would be with us (Matthew 18:20). New Testament churches make time for corporate prayer in their regular worship time. But most churches will also call special prayer gatherings to seek God's direction and intervention for special occasions. The early church did this. We can see one example of their gathering to pray for apostles who had been incarcerated for proclaiming Jesus in Acts 4.

Singing

We also know that the early church incorporated songs of worship and praise in their gatherings. This would have been something they brought over from their Jewish Temple worship. The church's practice of singing songs of worship is mentioned a couple of times in the New Testament (Ephesians 5:19, Colossians 3:16).

Mutual Support

Because the early church viewed themselves as a family, they treated each other that way, and supported each other, spiritually emotionally, and even physically. When Acts 2 reports that they met for fellowship, the

Greek word is 'koinoneia,' and it speaks of an interactive community of mutual support. It wasn't just surface conversation. It meant that they got to know each other on a deeper level, and that extended to taking care of each other's needs. They really meant it when they called each other brother and sister. They treated each other like family and believed they had a responsibility to care for one another.

These are things that a church does. When a church openly proclaims the gospel, baptizes those who respond, teaches the Bible accurately and practically, gathers faithfully and worships with sincerity, supporting one another with unconditional love and forgiveness, people in the world are attracted. Lost people crave the things a genuine New Testament church has to offer.

If it is focused on its mission and faithfully conducts itself as a New Testament church, it gains the attention of the lost world who begin to look for what is behind this incredible institution. The end result is that Jesus is lifted up and people are reconciled to God through him.

Opposition

But there are some things that churches are up against that can hinder their work, and even derail them from their mission. Just about everything that churches face today, we have recorded for us in the Bible in the book of Acts. Acts is all about the launching of and expansion of the early church. While we see the church accomplishing great things, we can also see her up against some strong opposition.

Persecution

From its earlier beginnings, there were those who opposed the message and mission of the church, and they did everything they could to stop her work. Beginning in chapter three, enemies of the church threatened church leaders with physical harm. They imprisoned church members, and eventually put some of the most outspoken and effective leaders to death. As churches multiplied and spread throughout the Roman world, many churches faced the prospect of alienation of her members from the job market, suffering economic disaster. Many more were imprisoned, banished from their homeland, and put to death in horrible torturous ways. Yet in all this, the church continued to grow rapidly. As Tertullian, an early church leader, wrote, "The blood of the saints is the seed of the church."

Hypocrisy

If there is a real God, there is also a real devil. And if there is a real devil, of course, he will do all he can to stop the church. Think of it, if you were the devil, what would you do in order to shut down the church? I think the most effective tool in his arsenal is infiltration. He will send those who will disrupt the church from the inside, or he will work overtime to promote hypocrisy within its ranks. He did this very early in the life of the Jerusalem church, and does so in churches today.

Read Acts 4:32-5:11. What did Ananias and Sapphira do wrong?

Why did God deal with this so harshly?

In what ways is hypocrisy a threat to the church today?

Division

The evil one worked hard to stop the effectiveness of the church. He used persecution, but the church continued to grow and the persecuted believers only scattered and planted new churches where they went. He infected church members and implanted hypocrisy in the church. But God rooted it out and the church continued to grow. Then, he returned to his arsenal and used another one of his most effective weapons, division among members of the body.

The word, "devil" literally means "divider." He will do his best to divide us…from God and one another. He works overtime to create division in the church.

It happened very early on. The disciples were even prone to division within their ranks while they were still with Jesus. And early on in the church movement, in Acts 6, while the church was moving forward and growing strong, a critical spirit and complaining among members began to divide one group of Christ-followers from another. After the episode in Acts 6, we can trace similar challenges in the church through the rest of the 1st century and then throughout Christian history.

What do we learn from 1 Corinthians 1:10-13 about this problem?

How does Paul say we should respond to divisive people in Romans 16:17-18?

What a Church Needs

This is the longest chapter in this book and there is a reason for it. Having a right attitude toward and involving yourself in a good Bible-teaching local church will be the key to your spiritual growth. The church is God's design for doing his work in this age. He wants to use the church in your life. But he also wants to use you to impact the church.

The church has everything it needs. It has Jesus at the center and he is its central message. It has the blessing of God, being the body of Christ. It has the Holy Spirit working in believers as they gather to worship God and do his work.

And yet, the church needs you. The church is made up of people, people who have been called out of the world to be God's special chosen people. That's you. God wants to use you in the church to make a difference and promote her work. God wants you to be a committed member of the body who not only receives, but also contributes to her well-being and helps accomplish the church's mission.

You need the church. And the church needs you.

Become a Member

For starters, make the commitment to the church that you are part of her, that you will be loyal to her, and that you will serve her. That's what church membership is. It's commitment.

We already talked about the Biblical roots to membership, joining a church is Biblical. If you have found a Bible-teaching church that is operating in a New Testament way and working toward accomplishing the mission Jesus gave it (reaching the lost), then what is hindering you from joining? When you join a church, you are simply saying, "This is my church. I'm going to do everything I can to protect this church, to promote this church, and to serve this church." Joining a church is simply saying that you are going to be to the church what God has called you to be.

Attend Faithfully

Remember, the meaning of the Greek word for church is "assembly." You are not really "in a church" if you are not gathering with the other church members. Being part of the body means being with them. For the early Christians, they met together every chance they could. For them, their weekly gatherings were a privilege, and even when under persecution they met together weekly, and even more often than that, despite the threat it brought them.

Hebrews 10:24-25 says – "Let us consider how to stir up one another to love and good works, not neglecting to meet together, as is the habit of some, but encouraging one another, and all the more as you see the Day drawing near."

Like everything else in life, faithfully attending church or regularly skipping church becomes a habit. Develop the habit of attending every week. Even when traveling and out of town, check out a local church in the place you are visiting. What a wonderful blessing to be able to meet other followers of Jesus in other parts of the country or world.

Serve Sacrificially

Church is not a show, it's a family. One of the best ways to feel that you belong is by involving yourself and serving faithfully. Find a ministry in the church where your gifts and passions can be put to use for God's Kingdom and pour yourself into it. You might be surprised by the lifelong friends you make when you are part of a ministry team. Working shoulder to shoulder with others to accomplish something you both really believe in builds a strong sense of camaraderie and serves as a foundation to deep relationships. The sacrifices you make to put time and effort into God's kingdom will pay off in temporal and eternal dividends (Galatians 6:9).

Support Financially

Generosity is something that is talked about throughout Scripture and something that Jesus himself encouraged often. It's such an important aspect of Christian life and growth that I've included a larger section on it in a later chapter. For followers of Jesus, we should be generous to those causes that matter most to him. And what matters more to Jesus than the mission of his church? If we are receiving benefit from our church, it's very important that we support it, so that the church can continue to make a difference in other people's lives, as well.

Practice Love

Because the church is full of people, you'll have plenty of opportunity to put Christian love into practice. While churches are filled with wonderful people, they're still people, they're still sinners. You will get offended.

You'll witness hypocrisy. These people might be saved, but they are still struggling with their own sin and selfishness, just like you are. So, in the church family, we have opportunity to love the way Jesus taught us, to forgive, to be patient, to be kind in the face of offense, to love the unlovely, and to care for and help bear the burdens of struggling people. Jesus told his followers that this is how people will know that we are genuinely following him.

Encourage Unity

As we saw earlier, the Divider will do all he can to create division and disharmony in the church. If you are actively involved in a church, you'll undoubtedly overhear murmuring by some and gossip by others (usually the same people). When that happens, you have the responsibility to confront the work of the devil (he often works through good people, i.e. Peter in Matthew 16:23) by pursuing peace and building unity. It usually isn't enough to simply keep quiet. Being a peacemaker and building unity often takes active and intentional intervention. Sometimes a simple and kind response expressing support for the church or the person being criticized is all that is necessary. Sometimes you may have to bring the matter to a church leader. But it's the responsibility of everyone in the church body to keep it healthy and united around Jesus' Great Commission.

Being an active participant in a local church can be one of the greatest blessings of your Christian life. But the level of that blessing is largely up to you. Understanding what the church is, how precious it is to God, the gravity of the work she has been called to do, and the force of opposition she is up against, will help us realize all that is at stake. And in the end, the blessings we receive from the church are proportional to the blessings we give to the church. We will get from it what we put into it. So, join, attend faithfully, serve, love, and promote peace and unity.

Because when God saved you, he saved you as an individual, but he saved you to be part of his family.

CHAPTER 8

Learn God's Word

By now, you've become at least somewhat familiar with the Bible. In every one of these chapters, we've looked up a number of Bible passages. If you've been attending a church like mine, you've learned that Christians put a lot of emphasis on understanding and applying principles taught in the Bible.

I'm sure you've also heard a lot of things about the Bible outside of church as well, some negative and maybe some positive. Secularists want to malign it and denounce its teachings. Many religious people try to twist its words into supporting what they want it to say. As Jesus-followers, we believe what it says and encourage each other to practice its teachings.

But what of it? Is it really reliable? Can we trust a book that was written over 2,000 years ago? And if we can trust its accuracy and reliability, how can we understand something that was written in and to such different cultures from our own? That's what this chapter is about. How can we know that the Bible is trustworthy and how can we study its contents to understand them and apply to our lives?

Let's start with just a basic overview of the Bible, how it is composed and who actually wrote it. And of course, what is the subject matter? Why it was written.

Authorship

The Bible, as we are familiar with it today, may look like a book, but it's not really. It's actually a collection of a lot of books, sixty-six in all. And it was written by a bunch of authors, forty, in fact.

Who were these people? Well, they were men from all walks of life and from different parts of the ancient mid-eastern world, from cultures separated by as many as fifteen hundred years. Some were rich, some very poor. Some were powerful kings, others were on the run for their lives. They were prophets, patriarchs, and common people.

But what's really interesting is that these guys, though they were from such diverse backgrounds, and though they wrote about a very wide variety of subjects, many of which were controversial then as today, they agreed with each other, 100% of the time. And that's amazing!

Authors included well-known Bible characters, such as Moses, Joshua, David, Solomon, Jeremiah, Daniel, John, Peter, and Paul. And it also included some people you probably haven't heard of, like Habakkuk, Haggai, or Jude. But whether or not you've heard of them, all of these authors were well known in their day and highly respected. They were viewed as men of God, and it was believed by the people who knew them and read their books, that they were speaking on behalf of God. That's why the books they wrote were preserved, copied, and distributed. The people of their day viewed their writings as being sacred, and in a special way, inspired by God.

That brings us to another level of this discussion about the authorship of the books of the Bible. Was God involved in producing and preserving these books? Were they merely human compositions, or were they productions of God himself, using human agents?

The authors themselves believed that there was more to their writing than just their own ideas. They repeatedly claimed to be speaking for God with phrases such as, "Thus says the Lord."

Old Testament

By the time Jesus came along, the Jews had collected thirty-nine books that they viewed as the Word of God in written form (see chapter one on "Special Revelation"). Together, these books made up the Mikra (meaning "Readings") and are today known by Jews as the Tanakh, which is an acronym using the first Hebrew letter for each of the sections in their Bible: Torah ("Teaching"), Nevi'im ("Prophets"), and Ketuvim ("Writings"). This is the same collection of books that Christians call the Old Testament. In Jesus' day, this group of sacred books was viewed as a complete collection of their authoritative Scripture. It is quite clear from Jesus' teaching that he also viewed this collection of books as more than the words of the human authors, but as the authoritative Word of God.

Look up Matthew 22:43. Jesus quotes from King David in the Psalms. How does he say that David knew what to write?

Read Matthew 5:17-18. How did Jesus view the Law (Torah) and the Prophets?

In John 10:35, what does Jesus call the Scripture?

Based on Matthew 4:4, 7, 10, how does Jesus view Old Testament Scripture?

According to Matthew 12:40 and Matthew 24:37, how did he view the supernatural stories in the Bible, as true occurrences or fables?

Based on Luke 24:46-47 and John 5:39, what did Jesus believe the Old Testament Scriptures pointed to?

So, it is clear that Jesus believed that the Jewish Tanakh, or the Christian Old Testament, was divine in origin and to be believed and obeyed as God's Word.

That's the first and largest section of the Bible. The last book of this collection had been written and the books were assembled about four hundred years before Jesus came.

New Testament

But everything that we know about Jesus' life, death and resurrection is from the second major section of the Bible, what we call the New Testament. It is clear from the writers of the New Testament that they believed the Old Testament was divinely inspired Scripture. However, these same

New Testament authors also believed that God had fulfilled the teachings of the Old Testament through Jesus, as the Messiah. They were convinced that in the same way that the Old Testament books were divinely inspired, they were now being led and directed by God to record the life, teachings, miracles, and works of Jesus, as well as introduce teachings that flowed from his life, death and resurrection.

Look up 2 Peter 3:15-16. What New Testament author does Peter refer to in the passage?

To what does he compare Paul's writings to toward the end of v. 16?

Read 1 Timothy 5:18. Paul has two quotations in this verse. What are they?

Before he quotes them, what does he say they are?

The first quotation is from the Old Testament book, Deuteronomy. The second is a quotation from Luke's Gospel, Luke 10:7. What does this tell us about Paul's view of Luke's writings?

The New Testament is made up of 27 books. Four of them are biographies of Jesus during the time of his ministry. One is a written documentary on how Jesus' Apostles launched the early church after Jesus' resurrection. The rest are letters that Paul and a couple of Jesus' disciples wrote to churches and Christians about the gospel and living the Christian life. The last book, Revelation, is a prophecy about the end times.

As I mentioned earlier, the New Testament authors themselves had a high regard for Scripture, and believed that the words of Scripture were given in a supernatural way, through divine inspiration.

Read 2 Timothy 3:16-17. How does Paul the Apostle say Scripture came to us?

What does he say Scripture is profitable for?

Look up 2 Peter 1:21. Did Peter believe Scripture came as the ideas of men?

How does he say Scripture came to us?

So, Old Testament authors, Jesus, and New Testament authors believed that the writing of Scripture was very special, supernatural in fact. Paul's words in 2 Timothy 3:16 say that Scripture was "breathed by God" as in breathed into the men he was directing to write the words of Scripture. Jesus' close friend, Peter, said, literally, that men, who were set aside by God in a special way, were "moved along and guided by the Holy Spirit" (2 Peter 1:21).

Yet, we see different writing styles and personalities in the individual books. The men who wrote the Bible books used their native languages, their vocabulary, their education, and their personality. We see a pretty big difference in style between the Apostle Paul and the Apostle John. If it was all inspired by God, why the differences?

Inspiration does not mean dictation.

Some of Jesus' words to his disciples can be helpful here, especially when you consider that these guys would oversee the writing and transmission of the New Testament text, and afterward call it "Scripture" (2 Peter 3:15-16).

Read John 14:25-26. Who does Jesus promise to send to the disciples?

What does he say the Holy Spirit will do for them?

Now read John 16:12-15. What does Jesus tell his apostles about the work that the Holy Spirit will play in their future ministries?

Read again 2 Peter 1:21. How does Peter's explanation of Scripture enlighten Jesus' promise in these two passages?

So, in these passages, Jesus tells his disciples that the Holy Spirit would reveal things to them. He tells them that the Holy Spirit would bring to their memories Jesus' words (the Gospels), that he would teach them things related to Jesus' work (the Epistles), and that he would tell them about things yet to come (Revelation).

These words of Jesus served as a foundation for the early church to insist that for any book to be considered as New Testament Scripture, it had to have a connection with one of the Apostles, who had been given this promise by Jesus.

Also from these passages, we get insight into the way the Holy Spirit inspired Scripture. He brought to their memory those things they should record. He taught them principles that they were to teach. And he would let them in on future events that they should pass on.

But he did not dictate the words to them, the way you might dictate into your smartphone for voice texting.

Instead, he put into their minds the things they should write, allowing their personalities, language, vocabulary, and life experience to shape the way those truths would be presented. But in overseeing the writing itself, he influenced the very words that they chose, ensuring their accuracy, and approving all that was written.

Throughout church history, Christians have held to what we call "verbal plenary" inspiration of the Scriptures. "Verbal" means "words" and "plenary" means "as a whole" or "every." In other words, the historical Christian position on the inspiration of Christian Scriptures is that every word is inspired by God, and that as a whole, it is God's inerrant infallible Word.

That tells us something about the authorship of the Old and New Testament books, and how the Holy Spirit worked through special people to produce divinely inspired and authoritative Scripture.

But a question that often gets asked is, who decided what books were actually inspired by God and were to be included in the Bible?

Why those 66

For the Old Testament, it happened long before Jesus came into the picture. As the books were being written, priests of Jehovah (Yahweh) set them aside because of their sacred nature. About 400 years before Jesus, Jewish priests settled on the 39 books of the Jewish Scriptures (Christian Old Testament) as divinely inspired Scripture. We've already seen that Jesus accepted the Old Testament as God's Word. Being followers of Jesus, since he accepted those books, we do as well.

The New Testament text was settled pretty early in the Christian era. Some books were universally accepted as being inspired Scripture while the Apostles were still alive. We saw that earlier when the Apostle Peter referred to Paul's letters as Scripture, and Paul referring to Luke's Gospel as Scripture.

By the end of the second century, churches around the Roman world had universally settled on our current 27 New Testament books as Christian Scriptures. They believed that these books rested upon the foundation of the Old Testament, and that the Old Testament pointed to Jesus, while the New Testament books recorded and explained the teaching and work of Jesus.

There are letters, sermons and articles written by early church fathers in those first few centuries that show us something of the process early church leaders (pastors of churches from around the Roman world) used to determine which books were actually written by Apostles. These books were therefore in fulfillment of Jesus' statements in John 14 and 16, that we looked at earlier.

In order for the early church to accept New Testament books to be authentic Scripture, they insisted that the books...

- Be written by an Apostle or the writing be overseen by an Apostle (one who was a witness of Jesus' resurrection and commissioned by Jesus personally to take the gospel to the world). This was in fulfillment of John 14:25-26 and John 16:12-15.
- Be spiritually and factually compatible with the teachings of the Old Testament and the Christian tradition that had been passed on to them from the Apostles.
- Be universally and independently accepted by churches around the world at that time as an indication of the leading of the Holy Spirit.
- Demonstrate internal evidence of divine inspiration.

The New Testament books we have today were almost universally accepted in their current form by virtually all the independent churches around the world by the close of the second century. Contrary to popular quasi-historical fiction authors, no council or Roman emperor had any influence in determining which books were to be included in the New Testament and which books were not. The Council of Carthage towards the end of the fourth century ratified what the early church leaders had been claiming for two hundred years before that time. But the acceptance of the 66 books of the Bible deemed "canonical" had already taken place. This process was one that happened organically. The fact that thousands of churches separated by thousands of miles all came to the same conclusions as to which books were canonical speaks of the work of the Holy Spirit giving them universal yet independent direction.

I'd like to say something briefly about sensational reports of "lost books" of the Bible, or books that were supposedly censored by religious elites back in the day. In truth, none of these books were lost. Scholars and Christian leaders have known about them for centuries, and I've personally read many of them. They were rejected for good reason. None were early works. Books such as the Gospel of Judas, the Epistle of Barnabas, or the Gospel of Mary Magdalene were universally rejected in their day and also by modern scholars. They are called "pseudepigrapha" (meaning "false writing") because none were actually written by the purported author, and in fact, were products of a much later date, long after the Apostles had died, and most after the time of Constantine. They are interesting reads, but dramatically different in character from New Testament books. It takes only a cursory inspection to quickly determine that they are not anywhere in the same league as New or Old Testament books. But they periodically hit the news because sensationalism sells.

The books that we have in our New Testament today were carefully examined by the earliest Christians in light of all they had learned from the Apostles themselves, and they were universally accepted as divinely inspired writings for good reason.

So that, in a nutshell, is how the books of the Bible came to be accepted as authoritative Scripture among Christians around the world.

What are these books? What's in them, and why are they organized in the order they appear in our Bible?

Organization

Because the Bible is not a single book, but a collection of books, understanding how they are organized within the Bible is helpful. The Bible was not intended to be read from cover to cover, like a novel. Some portions of the Bible were not even intended to be read at all, but are reference materials, like law books, or genealogical records. I know that a lot of people want to read the Bible from beginning to end, each book in the order they appear in the Bible, from Genesis through Revelation, and there's nothing wrong with that. But it's not how the Bible was intended to be read or studied.

To get a better handle on how to read and study the Bible, let's take a brief look at how it's organized. We've already talked about the division between the Old Testament and the New Testament. Let's break it down further.

Old Testament	New Testament
History *(Genesis–Esther)*	**History** *(Matthew–Acts)*
Poetry *(Job–Song of Songs)*	**Paul's Epistles** *(Romans–Philemon)*
Major Prophets *(Isaiah–Daniel)*	**General Epistles** *(Hebrews–Jude)*
Minor Prophets *(Hosea–Malachi)*	**Revelation**

Random Facts

The Old Testament was written in Hebrew and the New Testament was written in Greek. Hebrew was the spoken and written language of the Israelites, and it was close enough in form to their neighboring nations that many outside of Israel could also understand it if they had access to it.

When Israel was defeated by the Babylonians (600 BC), they were scattered and Jewish settlements appeared all over the Mediterranean world. Gentiles (anyone who is not a Jew) were intrigued with the Tanakh and it began to receive wider attention. Because of Alexander the Great's conquests (330BC), the Greek language became the universal language of commerce in the Mediterranean world. Educated people were gaining interest in the Hebrew Scriptures so a translation of the Old Testament into

Greek known as the Septuagint, was made in Alexandria, Egypt. But the original language of the Old Testament was Hebrew.

That's important because it helps us understand the obscure nature of some passages. Hebrew is a very picturesque language and words do not have the same precise meaning that they do in Greek, or even English. In order for an accurate translation to be made of the original Hebrew text, it's necessary to know the context of the passage and the culture surrounding its writing. Modern English translations do a good job in making it understandable for us today, while preserving the accuracy of what was originally written.

It's helpful to know that scholars today have great confidence in the transmission (meaning "passed on from the original" – the ancient copies that are available today) of the Old Testament text. Although it had been copied many times over, when very early pre-Christian copies of it have been discovered, they contain virtually the same text as much later copies. Those who oversaw the transmission of sacred documents had such reverence for the text, and their work was checked and rechecked by others, that mistakes were incredibly rare.

The New Testament was written in Greek. Greek is a much more precise language than Hebrew, and even English. Because a lot of ancient Greek literature exists, we also have a clear understanding of the language and how it can be accurately translated. Because of the nature of the language, important concepts of doctrine regarding Jesus and the gospel were carefully communicated in the New Testament, and we can be certain of the concepts being explained as they were originally written.

As with the Old Testament, we can also have great confidence that the New Testament we have today is essentially what the original authors wrote. While hundreds of years, in some cases more than a thousand years, separate other ancient documents (i.e. Iliad and Odyssey of Homer, Caesar's Gallic Wars) from their original copy, we have portions of New Testament copies that were made only decades after their original writing. Some may even be first generation copies. When historians explain the process that professional scribes went through to ensure the accuracy of their copies, it gives us great confidence that the Bible we have today is essentially what the ancients had in their day, when the Holy Spirit originally inspired the authors to write.

So, although you often hear people saying something like, "The Bible has been copied so many times and translations made of translations, there's no way to know what was originally in it," you can know that is just not true. The copies were extremely accurate, and the English translations we have today were translated directly from accurate copies that were in the language it was originally written in. The Bible we have today is essentially what was inspired by the Holy Spirit.

The Old Testament contains 39 books, 929 chapters and 23,214 verses. Psalms is the longest book and Obadiah is the shortest. If you open an average Bible (without extensive study notes) in the middle, you will probably open it to Psalms.

The New Testament contains 27 books, 260 chapters, and 7,959 verses. Acts is the longest book and 2 John is the shortest. Not only are there fewer New Testament books, they are much shorter books. While there are roughly 1/3 the number of verses in the New Testament, those verses are also shorter than most verses in the Old Testament. The New Testament is actually less than 1/4 the length of the Old Testament. That's mainly because the Old Testament contains lengthy genealogies, detailed case law for the nation of Israel, an entire song book for their worship (Psalms), and thousands of years of history. The New Testament contains history, but is able to get right to the point with the gospel of Jesus and practical Christian living, also making it much easier in the ancient world to disperse among churches around the world in a day when mass communication was more difficult.

Survival

Something else that points to the supernatural nature of the Bible is its uncanny survival in a world that has attacked its message, opposed its existence, and ridiculed its contents.

Attempts to destroy the Tanakh (the Jewish Bible and Christian Old Testament) began very early. Two hundred years before Jesus, a Seleucid ruler named Antiochus Epiphanes conquered Palestine and ordered all copies of Jewish Scriptures to be burned. Anyone found with a copy of Jewish Scripture was put to death. Still, the Bible survived.

In the early days of Christianity, persecution under the Romans was, at times, intense. The Emperor Diocletian, in 303 AD, ordered all copies of Christian Scriptures to be destroyed. Yet, the Bible not only survived, it was prolifically copied and distributed, nearly overwhelming the Roman Empire to the place where, a few years after Diocletian, the emperor Constantine was compelled to legalize Christianity.

Following Constantine, one more emperor arose who attempted to stamp out Christianity and destroy all of their Scriptures. This was the Emperor Julian. But even as he was publishing and distributing his own written tirade against the Bible, copies of that Bible were proliferated and disseminated throughout his empire at a record pace.

Over the centuries, there have been many attempts to prohibit the copying and distribution of the Bible. There have been laws decreed making the translation of the Bible into a common language a criminal offense, and translators of the Bible have been martyred. In some parts of the world even in modern times, translating or owning a copy of the Bible is prohibited (i.e. China). In the west today, there have been many academic and intellectual attacks against the Bible, but all eventually come to nothing. It is the most translated and most read collection of books around the world.

I think of the French philosopher Voltaire (18th century), who predicted the death of Christianity by the end of his lifetime and claimed the Bible was obsolete and soon to be out of print. Today, it is unusual to ever see a copy of anything Voltaire wrote, while the Bible is still the number one selling book worldwide every year. Shortly after his death, Voltaire's own office was converted into a Bible depository, where copies of Scripture were stored from floor to ceiling.

Similar attempts are made to discredit the Bible in modern academia and popular media. But despite common claims that the Bible contains errors and contradictions, we can dismiss those claims by honestly studying the context of the passage, its literary genre, the author's intent, and the understanding of the original readers.

I've often been personally told that there are contradictions and errors in the Bible. Each time I've asked the person making the statement to show me one. No one has yet been able to do so. Usually, people making this statement are only repeating what they've heard, but have not studied it themselves to see if those claims are compelling.

Certainly, not everything in the Bible can be explained. And while archeology and science from time to time present theories that seem to contradict what is said in the Bible, in the end, the Bible always shows itself to be trustworthy.

Usefulness

The Bible is a great and special book. But like an unwrapped gift, its purpose is not to be a mere beauty to be revered. If the Bible is to be anything to us, it must be studied, learned and applied.

We looked at 2 Timothy 3:16 earlier. Read it again. After declaring Scripture to be God-breathed, what does Paul tell Timothy that the Bible is useful for?

Explain what you believe each of those four words mean and how that helps us today?

Reading and studying the Bible helps us understand God. God has revealed himself to us through his Word. So, by reading his Word, we get to know him.

The Bible also helps us to understand life. Reading God's Word gives us an outside view, a perspective from a distance. When we see life from God's vantage point, things that otherwise would never make sense, come into focus.

I grew up in La Crosse, Wisconsin, a beautiful small city nestled between tall rock faced bluffs and the Mississippi River. The prominent outcroppings that towered above the city were a constant invitation to me as a boy, and as soon as I was old enough to ride my banana seat bike around town without supervision, my friends and I were climbing and exploring those bluffs. We'd bring packs and gear that we bought from the army surplus store, and make a whole day of it.

The most intriguing to me was the cave I could see on the second largest of the bluffs called "Indian Joe's" (I think from Mark Twain's *Tom Sawyer*). It was easily visible from my bedroom window and from just about anywhere in the city. But my friends and I climbed that bluff twice, and spent hours looking without finding the cave. We became disoriented once we got up on the rocks. Everything looked the same and we could not figure out why we couldn't reach our intended destination. We descended near sundown both times, disappointed and wondering if our eyes had been playing tricks on us.

Then I got an idea. From the ground, I could see exactly how to get to the cave. I had gotten a black and white Polaroid camera for my birthday that year. So, I took a picture of the cave from the ground, and a friend and I climbed the 500 feet or so up to the rocky face. I pulled the picture out of my pocket and by using a couple of identifiable trees and ledges that coincided with them, we were able to navigate straight to the cave.

It was the first time I understood the phrase, "Can't see the forest for the trees." When you are in the middle of something, it's hard to know what direction to go to get where you want to be. We get lost in detail when we don't see the big picture. That's how it was for us as kids on Indian Joe's bluff. We never knew where we were on the rocky face in relation to the cave. But when we were able to use the picture as a guide, we went straight to it.

That's why Proverbs 29:18 says, "Where there is no vision, the people perish." Vision here refers to direction from God. The New Living Translation puts it like this, "Without revelation people run wild; but one who listens to instruction will be happy."

This life can quickly turn into chaos and confusion. It's only through God's Word and following his direction and instructions, that the mess of information before our eyes becomes untangled, enabling us to see the right path clearly.

Read Psalm 119:105. What does he compare God's Word to here?

Ultimately, when we get to know and understand God, we then see life from his perspective. Thus, we gain a new understanding of life, which enables us to follow him, and fulfill the purpose that we were created for, which is to please him. If it were not for God's Word, we could not know what he expects of us, how we can please him and what honors and glorifies him. But by reading his Word, we learn who he is, how he wants us to live, and how we can please him.

Read

Sadly, a lot of Christians rarely, if ever, read the Bible. If we believe that God's Word is like a lamp that lights our path in life (Psalm 119:105), that we learn about God and what he expects of us in this life through Scripture, it seems that we would want to know what it actually says. That means we have to read it. Here are some things that will help you get into the habit of reading the Bible with understanding.

Set aside time every day.

Most of us do not meet with God regularly because we don't make the appointment. I've learned that I need to have a time set aside every morning to read God's Word. I'm not talking about an hour or even a half hour. Just set aside 15 to 20 minutes every day to read the Bible. You'll be surprised how much you will get through in a month's time if you do it every day. So, make an appointment. Put it in your smartphone calendar with an alarm. Read it the same time every day.

Have a plan.

You don't want to simply pick the Bible up and start reading randomly wherever it opens. That wouldn't be the best way to learn what's really inside.

Here's my suggested plan to help you get started: start reading in the book of Matthew. Read all about Jesus' life and teaching, his death and resurrection, and then his Great Commission. Once you finish Matthew (you can get through a couple of chapters every day in just 15 minutes), go back and read it again. It's better to really get to know one book, rather than reading a lot and not really getting it. So, read Matthew through a couple of times.

After Matthew, read Ephesians. When you finish Ephesians, read it again, and again. Ephesians is a great example of Paul's epistles, but it's not as long as, say, Romans. In the beginning chapters, you get some very interesting doctrine explained. In the closing chapters, you get a lot about practical Christian living.

After reading Ephesians a few times, read the Book of Luke. Notice the things in Luke that you remember from Matthew, and pay attention to those things that are new, or from a different perspective. After Luke, read Acts (written by Luke and a continuation of his Gospel). Then go back and read Ephesians again. This time, you'll have a lot more insight after Luke and Acts.

Starter Bible Reading Plan
Matthew (read twice through)
Ephesians (read three times through)
Luke (once through)
Acts (twice through)
Ephesians again
John (twice through)
Romans (twice through)
Genesis (twice through)
Mark
Philippians (three times through)
Exodus (skim genealogies and laws–they are for reference)
Acts again
Colossians (three times through)
Leviticus & *Numbers* (again skim the genealogies and laws)
1 & 2 Thessalonians (twice through)

By the time you get this far, you are well underway in understanding how to read the Bible. You could either pick up another Bible reading plan (they are easy to find online), or you can get The Bridge Church's reading plan. It's published monthly and available in booklet form, as well as online (thebridge.church/readingplan).

Take notes.

Dawson Trotman, founder of The Navigators, used to say, "Thoughts untangle themselves over the lips and through the fingertips."

As you are reading, take notes. You'll get a lot more out of it, and you'll remember a lot more of what you read. Write down the things that you learn that you didn't know before. Write down the things that seem to speak to you, things that you sense God wants you to work on in your life, or ways the Word is encouraging you. Write out important verses that you want to know and practice better. This is why I've had questions throughout this book, to show you the value of writing down your thoughts, understanding and application of Scripture.

Stay with it.

"The godly may trip seven times, but they will get up again." – Proverbs 24:16 NLT

You might get going and read for several days straight, but then miss a couple of days. Whether or not reading the Bible becomes a lifestyle for you depends on what you do when you miss. Will you become discouraged and quit? Or will you get back to it again, and resume working on it as a daily habit?

Study

We read the Bible so that we can learn. But reading it is just the beginning. To really get to know the Bible, you have to study it. Studying

Scripture is best done in a group, with other believers, a teacher or mentor of some sort, with some background material on the book you are studying.

Most local churches have plenty of opportunities to do a study with a few others. There is something about group participation that helps with accountability and cements in the mind the things we are learning. So, seek out a group in your church that has a meeting time that will work in your schedule. If your church doesn't offer anything at a time that works for you, seek out *Bible Study Fellowship*, a nondenominational ministry that meets all over the country, usually in churches (though not affiliated with any church). Their studies are super helpful and a great way to connect with other Christians.

If studying with a group is not possible, I'd suggest you pick up *Living By The Book* by Howard Hendricks. It's a great simple book that walks you through studying the Bible on a deeper level.

You may also want to purchase a good study Bible. I recommend, *The ESV Study Bible.* It's available in print, as a smartphone or tablet app, and online. I have all three. Another helpful study Bible that takes a more practical and easier to understand approach is *The NLT Life Application Study Bible.*

Read Psalm 1. What kind of man does David say is blessed?

He starts with three negatives, and each one progresses. How so?

Instead, what does the blessed man delight in?

What does this blessed man do day and night?

What is the result? What metaphor does David use of him? Why is that fitting?

Read Joshua 1:8. In a shorter fashion, this verse teaches something similar. What does Joshua say will bring success?

Both Psalm 1 and Joshua 1:8 are teaching general principles, and do not guarantee health and economic success to people who meditate on God's Word. And success in the Bible is different from our culture's understanding of it. Success from God's perspective is doing what he created us to do in a way that pleases him, positively affecting others, and bringing personal fulfillment. Usually, that kind of success has nothing to do with having lots of money, which tends to be our American understanding.

In both of these passages, the emphasis is "meditating" on God's Word. When we think of meditation, we may think of Eastern mysticism, like transcendental meditation. That's not what this is. That kind of meditation is an emptying of the mind. But meditation in the Bible is a filling of the mind with God's Word. It is pondering, considering, thinking about every facet, and planning ways to incorporate the Scripture into one's life.

There were a lot of cows where I grew up. Cows have four compartments in their stomach. When they are out in the pasture, they grab as much grass and hay as they can and swallow it quickly, sending it down to the first compartment, barely chewing it. There, the juices in the stomach begin to soften the stalks. When they are back in their barn stall with nothing to do, they bring that hay from the first compartment back up to their mouths (I know, it's the gross part, but hear me out) and begin chewing on it. It's called, "chewing their cud." Because the grass has been softened, they are able to get rich nutrition out of the stalks that wasn't available to them when they first ate it. As they chew, they send the cud down to the second compartment of their stomach, where stomach acids break it down further. Later, they bring it up again and repeat the process. In the end, every little bit of nutrition is pulled out of the grass and hay that they ate. And that giant cow can be nutritionally sustained from grass and hay alone.

You and I could never survive on such a meager diet. And it's because we don't have a digestive system that is able to pull nutrition out of such a scant source. But cows and sheep and other ruminating animals are able to, because they "ruminate" (the scientific term for chewing their cud).

That's why the word "meditate" is synonymous with "ruminate." Because when you meditate on something, you pull every bit of good from whatever it is that you are thinking about.

God wants us to do that with his Word. He wants us to ponder it, meditate on it, ruminate on it. He wants us to pull every bit of value from his life-giving Word and digest it into our lives.

It's not that the act of meditating on God's Word makes God happy so that he does good things for us. Instead, God's Word has God's blessing on it, because it's his Word. So when we fully incorporate his Word into our lives, by mediation and application, the blessing that is on his Word, becomes a part of our lives.

Think of the Bible like you would an owner's manual. If you follow the manual, you will have success with the item, it will work well for you and will be useful, and it will last a long time. But if you ignore the manual, you'll probably end up with a breakdown.

God's blessing is associated with his principles, his spiritual laws. Just like keeping natural laws (i.e. gravity) bring about prosperity, and ignoring them brings physical pain and even death, keeping God's spiritual laws is beneficial for us.

So, by pondering, meditating, and applying God's principles, we bring the blessing that is connected to those principles into our lives.

I've also practiced a simple form of daily Bible study for years, that incorporates memorization and meditation. I've taught it to many people who have found it to be beneficial. Here it is:

1. Choose a passage. I suggest a dozen or so verses, like 1 Corinthians 13.
2. Every morning, as soon as you get up, read the whole passage (whole chapter in this case) out loud. (Reading it out loud makes your brain work twice as hard.)
3. Write out your verse of the day (one verse) on a 3x5 card, or type it into your phone so that you can carry it with you. Using a study Bible, or an online commentary, make some notes about that verse that help you to understand it more and apply it better.
4. Commit that verse to short-term memory. In other words, repeat it over and over out loud, until you can say it just one time without looking at it.
5. Carry the verse with you all day, and refer to it throughout the day (hourly). I use a trigger, such as getting up from my desk. Every time I stand, I pull the verse out and read it again, and think about what it means, and what I should be doing because of it. I think about how it should affect my job, my marriage, my kids and friendships.
6. At the end of the day, right before bed, read the whole passage through again, out loud.

If you do this, you'll be surprised how the entire passage will be committed to your memory, without you having to work on memorizing it. By repeating the whole passage out loud twice a day, and learning each individual verse so well through each day, your brain will begin to absorb the whole passage. And you'll not just know what the passage says, you'll know how to put it into use in your life. And because you're practicing what the Bible says, you'll bring the blessing of these principles into your life.

Apply

The point of reading, studying, and meditating, is so that you can understand the Word so well that you apply it to your life. Reading will do you no good if you do not apply it. Studying will do you no good if you do not apply it. Even meditating will do you no good if you do not apply it. The objective is application. God wants you to incorporate his Word, his principles, his law, into your life. In this way, in a sense, you become a living Bible for people to observe.

Read Joshua 1:8 again. After Joshua tells the people they should meditate on God's law, he says, "so that…" what?

Read Matthew 7:24-27. These are the closing words of Jesus' great "Sermon on the Mount." Fill in the blank:

"Everyone then who hears these words of mine and _____

_____…"

What will that person be like?

What is Jesus saying about the importance of applying God's Word?

How do you actually do that? There are two questions that every one of us should be asking ourselves as we are reading the Word, hearing it preached, or meditating on it.

1. *"How should my **thinking** change?"*

2. *"How should my **behavior** change?"*

As you are asking these two questions, be honest, even where it's hard. How you answer these questions and what you do as a result, will determine whether or not you receive the blessing that comes from applying God's Word.

Commit to thinking and behaving according to God's principles. That's application. That's what David meant when he said, "His delight is in the law of the Lord." That's what Jesus referred to as, "doing these sayings of mine."

So, we have learned that the Bible is an amazing collection of books. It is supernatural in character, uncanny in accuracy, and absolutely trustworthy. But it does us no good if we do not read it, study it, and apply it.

How are you going to apply this chapter?

What time of the day can you set aside every day to begin reading God's Word?

Will you do it?

CHAPTER 9

Talk With Your Creator

L ike many aspects of the Christian life, prayer is something many people misunderstand. A lot of people think of prayer as trite religious poems that are either read or recited in church services. Many remember bedtime or table prayers that were taught to them as children.

But praying in the Bible was very different from this. When people in the Bible prayed, they just talked to God. They didn't read anything or memorize anything. There are no examples anywhere in Scripture of anyone repeating a prayer. Every prayer in the Bible was original. They were all unique. The words didn't rhyme and they certainly didn't repeat the same phrases over and over. In the Bible, people prayed by talking to God. That's what prayer is. It is simply talking to God and believing that He is listening.

Proverbs 15:8 says, "The prayer of the upright pleases [God]" (NIV). God wants us to talk with him. When you think about it, we were created for that very purpose. If you remember from chapters 3, 4 and 5, God created us to enjoy a relationship with us. We know that sin wrecked our connection with him, but Jesus' death and resurrection made a way for us to be reconciled. Now, being saved, we are his children, and he wants us to get to know him more and more all the time. That can't happen without prayer. We can't have an ongoing and growing relationship with him if we do not interact with him, if we do not communicate with him. And that's what prayer is. Prayer is talking with God.

Prayer Makes a Difference

There are a lot of Scriptures that teach us that prayer also makes a difference in our lives. That God hears and answers prayer.

Read 1 Chronicles 16:11. This was written by King David. What was he urging all the people to do?

Look up Jeremiah 29:11. What promises regarding prayer are given here?

Read what Jesus said in Matthew 7:7-8. What three words does Jesus use to describe prayer here? And what do you think each refers to?

Read Philippians 4:6-7. Paul says prayer is useful to combat what?

What is the result of praying (with thanksgiving), according to verse 7?

What does Jesus tell his disciples to pray for in Matthew 9:37-38?

We could look up a lot more Scripture, but it is evident that the authors of the Bible really believed that prayer makes a difference and that God wants us to pray, and even commanded us to pray in a number of places (i.e. 1 Thessalonians 5:17). But they also taught that prayer is a way for us to see God change our circumstances, and in some cases, change the world. Jesus' half-brother, James, went so far as to say that many of us do not have things God wants us to have, because we do not ask him for them (James 4:2). So, prayer does make a difference.

It doesn't seem to work the way we want it to

But I don't see prayer always working that way. Most of us have prayed for some things that really mattered to us, and have not had those things happen in the way we prayed for them. A lot of us have prayed repeatedly for things only to be disappointed.

Have you ever wondered why some prayers seem to be answered and others do not? How come two guys pray for a job promotion and only one gets it? Does the other not have enough faith? What about the two couples who pray for pregnancy and one becomes pregnant, the other never does? Is God favoring the one couple over the other?

And there appears to be a major discrepancy between the big prayers that don't get answered and the little prayers that do. Recently, I've been praying for a woman in our church who has cancer. I keep praying and I know that she and her husband and kids keep praying, as well as a host of friends and family. But the news from tests and doctors is continually disappointing. However, the other day, I couldn't find my wallet. I prayed and kept looking, and sure enough, it seemed to show up in a remarkable way at a place where I never would have thought. God answered that prayer!

But the woman in our church still has cancer.

It doesn't seem like it should work that way, right?

I think that the main reason a lot of us rarely pray is because we've become discouraged with the results. We've not gotten what we've prayed for, and it's happened enough, that some of us have kind of quit praying.

Most will still say they believe in praying. Even the most discouraged among us still pray, at least once in a while. We think it helps...at least a little bit. So, a lot of people think of prayer like it's a "good luck charm." It's nice to have around, and we're sure it helps in some way. But few really believe in the power of prayer the way the authors of the Bible taught it. If we did, we'd pray a lot more.

A big misunderstanding

These problems point to a big misunderstanding about who God is and the nature of our relationship with him.

A lot of people view God as a fairy god-mother or personal genie who is supposed to be there to grant us our wishes. People wonder if they are not clicking their heels together hard enough, or maybe they are not rubbing the lamp just right. There are hucksters on TV promising people answered prayers if they purchase their special prayer cloth or send in a monetary donation to have the televangelist himself pray their requests. It all stems from a complete misunderstanding of the relationship God wants with us, and the nature of prayer.

Maybe a quick perusing of the first couple of chapters of this book would help. As you recall, God was not created for our benefit. We were created for him. He is not our fairy god-mother and talking to him is not a good luck charm. We are in existence to fulfill his wishes, not the other way around. Getting this wrong leaves us disillusioned and discouraged. It's the main reason a lot of people have given up on prayer. Because viewing God like he's supposed to be there for us turns us into the god and him into a minion. The very nature of sin itself is born of that aspiration. So, what we've done, then, is turn prayer into a sinful activity…requesting God to become our vassal and to do for us what we deem best.

But he's not going to play that way. He's God. We are his creation. We owe everything to him. He owes us nothing.

Prayer is not getting what we want from God. The very reason for our disillusionment with prayer comes from that misunderstanding, a misunderstanding that has its roots in our sin nature that Jesus died to deliver us from.

So now it's time for us to look at it from a different perspective, as children and servants of God, and not the other way around.

A great exchange

Does that mean we are not to open our hearts to God and express to him our deepest desires? Of course not! God wants to hear from us about everything. He wants us to pour out our longings, pain, needs and desires. He wants to hear it all from us. But he wants more than that.

The word in the New Testament for prayer is, "proseúxomai." It comes from two words, "pros" – "exchange" and "eúxomai" – "to wish." The word literally means to exchange wishes.

So, when you think of it, when Jesus taught his disciples how to pray, he started by saying, "Pray this way," or "Exchange wishes this way."

Here's what it means. Prayer is presenting our wants or desires (wishes) to God and giving them to him. But that's not all. It is then opening our hearts to receive his wants and desires (wishes). It's an exchange of wishes. We exchange our wishes for his.

I know that sounds risky. "What if I won't want what God wants?"

I committed my life to following Jesus when I was seventeen. I think I really meant it when I said, "Here God, take all of me." But after a while, I started to realize there were some things that I wanted and I wanted to hold on to them.

One area for me was girls. I wanted to date who I wanted to date. I didn't want to think about "God's will," when it came to girls. I thought I knew better. What if God wanted me to date an ugly girl with a boring personality? I wasn't willing to go there.

In my mind, it was like a game show. You know, where the contestant has a prize in hand, and he has to decide if he's willing to exchange it for something unknown behind a door. He can either keep what he has, or exchange it for something, he doesn't know what, behind that door. What will he do?

That was me as a Christian teenager. I knew what I liked in a girl. But if I gave all that to God, it was like exchanging what I had for some unknown entity behind a mystery door.

So, it was a lot easier for me to go to God and pray for what I wanted, or to use God like a personal genie — "Ok, God, I'm asking you to give me a good-looking blonde who laughs at my jokes and thinks I'm amazing." Those weren't my exact words, but they might as well have been.

Two problems with that. There was no faith involved. I didn't have to risk anything. I didn't have to trust God for his choice (or if he chose to keep me single). I could just demand that he give me what I want. That's a lot easier.

The other problem was that it put me in a bad state with God because I was treating him like the servant, and I was acting like the god. I was expecting him to do for me.

Do you see the problem?

As I spent more time praying, reading Scriptures, and hearing sermons, I began to realize what I was doing. I was dating girls, alright. But I wasn't growing in my relationship with God. That's when I made the exchange.

I still remember the night. I went to my knees and told God I was sorry. I told him what I was looking for in a girl, but that my desires were all messed up. I told him I'd rather trust him than me, and I was good with whatever/whoever he wanted. And I asked him to give me his desires, and to change my "wanter" to want what he wanted.

Today, I'm so glad I did. My kids are too. Because they would not have wanted some of the girls I had dated before for a mom! But they were blessed to have my wife, God's choice, as their mother.

God knew best all along. And even had he chosen to keep me single, his will is always best.

The best prayer life is one that not only recognizes this, but aims at it. It's exchanging our wishes for his.

How To Pray

Jesus' disciples had been amazed at a lot of things about Jesus. They were blown away by his miracles. But they never asked him to teach them how to do miracles. They were astonished by his teaching as he captivated crowds of thousands. Yet they never asked him to teach them how to preach.

But when they heard Jesus praying, they asked him to teach them how to pray (Luke 11:1-2). They knew that Jesus knew how to pray and they wanted to learn.

Here's the cool thing, they recorded for us what he taught them. It's clear from the Book of Acts that these guys learned it well and put it into practice. So, since we have the same lesson that he gave them, we have the same advantage that Jesus gave John, Peter, James, Matthew, and the other disciples.

So, let's look and see how Jesus taught his disciples to pray. Jesus' teaching on prayer is found in a couple of places in the Gospels, but let's look at what he says in Matthew 6:5-13.

> *"And when you pray, you must not be like the hypocrites. For they love to stand and pray in the synagogues and at the street corners, that they may be seen by others. Truly, I say to you, they have received their reward. But when you pray, go into your room and shut the door and pray to your Father who is in secret. And your Father who sees in secret will reward you.*
>
> *"And when you pray, do not heap up empty phrases as the Gentiles do, for they think that they will be heard for their many words. Do not be like them, for your Father knows what you need before you ask him.*
>
> *"Pray then like this: 'Our Father in heaven, hallowed be your name. Your kingdom come, your will be done, on earth as it is in heaven. Give us this day our daily bread, and forgive us our debts, as we also have forgiven our debtors. And lead us not into temptation, but deliver us from evil.'"*

How not to pray

Jesus started by telling them that there were some things they should not do when praying.

Then, as today, people had a misunderstanding of prayer. Most used it as an empty religious ritual and some to elevate themselves in the eyes of others. So, he told his followers things they were not to do.

He told them in v. 5 that they were not to pray like hypocrites. The word, hypocrite, was the Greek word for actor, or showman. He was saying that some people pray for show. They wanted others to see them praying, so that people thought of them as pious, or religious. Jesus says that the only reward for their praying would be the temporary reputation they received, but that nothing would come from God of their prayers.

Even today it is a temptation to pray for show. It's rare to see someone praying out in public in a boisterous fashion, the way the Pharisees of Jesus' day would do. But still, I think people do pray for show. It's easy for us to fall into the trap of crafting our public prayers in such a way that it sounds good to other people. In church circles, you sometimes hear people praying with flowery words, or adopting a prayer voice or prayer persona, using words or phrases they hear others using in their church circles.

The New Testament has many examples of people praying in a group, out loud together. And it's likely that they took turns praying out loud when they did. That's a good thing. We should be willing to pray out loud in a group and in front of others (refusing to do so can also be a matter of pride, just like praying for show is). But when we pray in front of others, it's very important that we simply talk directly to God, and not be worried about what others are thinking about our words or what we are saying.

I have this suggestion for you. As a new Christian, it might feel intimidating to pray out loud in a group setting (like in a Bible Study group, a ministry team, or a special church prayer gathering). But you can do it. The first couple of times, it's ok to simply listen to others praying and join with them in your heart. But don't be afraid to speak up and pray out loud also, not for the others, but to God. Here's a suggestion: start by praying just one or two sentences, until you begin to feel more comfortable. And talk directly to God. It might be as simple as, "God, thank you for being here and listening to us." Then next time, add a sentence or two.

The point that Jesus was making in this passage is that prayer is simply a conversation with God. It's just talking with him. So, we shouldn't go into any special prayer mode, or feel as though we have to say just the right words and even say them a certain way. That way of thinking keeps people from praying.

Prayer is a conversation. When we pray, we shouldn't talk any different than we normally do. I've been in some prayer gatherings where the people praying publicly sounded like they were yelling at God. They were all doing it so I could tell it was a special "prayer mode" in the culture of those people. But it's not what prayer is supposed to be. I've heard others pray who seem to always change their voice when they pray. They will sniffle and sound like they are crying. We shouldn't do that, unless we really are crying about something and talking to God about it. I've heard others change their voice inflections and begin to sound lofty or soft and spiritual. But when we pray, we shouldn't enter some special prayer mode with our voice or personality.

God just wants you to come to him as you are and for you to be yourself. Just talk to God.

In the second paragraph, or v. 7, Jesus says something else that we should not do. He says we should not use empty repetition, and pray in such a way that we are repeating the same words over and over, believing that there is some inherent value in the repetition of those words.

First century worship of false deities included rapid repeating of words over and over and over, believing the more they asked for something, the more power there was in the request. Jesus said that was nonsense, literally.

But I think this also applies to those who only pray by repeating memorized prayers without thinking about what they are saying. In order to avoid that danger and to make sure my mind is always engaged in what I am praying, I use my own words and simply talk to God. After all, that's how all the prayers in the Bible were. Even in this passage when Jesus gave the Lord's Prayer, he didn't tell us to memorize it and pray it word for word. He said, "Pray like this," or "Pray in this manner." It does not seem likely that he intended anyone to memorize his words and recite them like we do that Pledge of Allegiance, especially in light of his warning against using empty repetition.

Remember, prayer is just talking to God. That's what God wants you to do. Just talk to him.

Set a time and place

As he introduced how to pray, Jesus said a couple of times, "When you pray…"

That's actually really important. The reason a lot of people do not pray is because they do not have a time set aside to pray.

For Jesus' original audience, they understood this. It was part of the Jewish culture to have time set aside, three times a day, to pray. It was like they had three appointments with God, every day, to pray. Jesus didn't have to tell them to do that. They were already doing that. He was teaching them what to do during this time that was already set aside.

Have you heard of the story of Daniel in the Lion's Den? Daniel was thrown into a den of lions because he prayed three times a day to the one true God, and would not sacrifice his time of prayer, even when the King of Persia commanded him to stop. Daniel had an absolute time set aside for God, to pray, and it was supremely important to him. He was committed to that time and place for prayer, even though it meant that it could cost him his life. His reasoning was that his life was more dependent on God than anything else, even the King of Persia.

Do you think that way?

Do you have a time set aside that is for God, and God alone?

I found myself slipping in this area. Though I had a morning quiet time, I found that I would go through the rest of my day not thinking much of God's presence. And I'm a pastor! So, following the Jewish custom of Jesus' day, I decided to set aside a few minutes three times every day to pray. I set an alarm on my phone to remind me. Now every morning at 7a, every afternoon at 2p, and every night at 10p, my phone and my watch buzz and remind me to get with my Father in heaven for a few minutes. Like anything else in life, if I don't have a time set aside and remind myself, I don't do it.

But Jesus is even more insistent in his teaching about making a place for prayer. In verse 6 he says, "When you pray, go into your room and shut the door…"

The word for room is a special Greek word, meaning "inner room without windows." It was a closet. That's where the phrase, "prayer closet" comes from. Jesus was teaching his followers to make a special place where they pray.

There is something extra valuable about this. Having a place that is your special place for prayer makes a difference. When you make it a habit to go to that place to pray, every day, after a while, just entering that room or closet puts you into a prayer mindset. I think the way Jesus described it, it should be a place that protects you from distractions, where your mind is less likely to wander (I can't pray well in my office...I see books on my shelf that distract my thinking, etc.).

A lot of people tell me that they have their prayer time during their morning commute, or during some other mindless activity. I think it's great to pray while doing other things. But think about it, how good of a relationship would you have with your spouse if the only time you gave them was time you had available because you were doing other things? How special would he/she feel, if you rarely gave them undistracted time for just the two of you?

It's great to spend time with God while you are driving the car or folding the laundry. But God wants special committed time with you, when you are focused only on him. Doesn't he deserve it?

That's what having a special place for prayer does for us. It forces us to give time to him and him alone. And it catapults our prayer life to fulfillment beyond what we ever experienced before.

Where could you make a place for prayer? What could you refer to as your prayer closet? It could be a literal closet. That might be the best, and I have a number of friends who have a literal closet that they go into every day to spend time alone with God. I have a place at home and at work. Both places offer me privacy and help me to not be distracted.

So, before we go on, let's do that. Set a time and make a place for prayer. Let's do it now.

In light of this, when in your day can you make an appointment with God, for prayer?

What will you do to ensure that you become consistent in praying at that time?

What special place in your home can you set aside for your place of prayer?

Know who you are talking to

*"**Our Father in heaven**, hallowed be your name. Your kingdom come, your will be done, on earth as it is in heaven. Give us this day our daily bread, and forgive us our debts, as we also have forgiven our debtors. And lead us not into temptation, but deliver us from the evil one."*

Jesus began his lesson by saying, "Pray then like this: 'Our Father in heaven, hallowed be your name.'"

This isn't the only time Jesus told us to pray to the Father. He did this in a few places.

Read John 16:23. Who does Jesus say our prayers should be directed to?

In whose name does Jesus say we should pray?

Read Romans 8:26 and Jude 20. How does the Holy Spirit fit into our praying?

As you can see, the entire Trinity is involved in prayer. Jesus taught us to pray to the Father and he said to pray "in his name." To pray in Jesus' name means to pray, based on Jesus' credit. It's like having a cosigner for a loan. If you have no credit yourself when you request a loan, the bank will require you to have a cosigner, someone who has credit, in order to get that loan. You and I do not have the credit to ask the Father for anything. But Jesus does. He tells us to go to the Father based on his credit, in his name. So, the Father hears our petitions as though it were Jesus making them.

Jesus also promised his disciples the Holy Spirit, whom he called, "the Helper." In Romans 8:26, Paul pointed out how we often do not know how to pray or what to pray for. It is the Holy Spirit who helps us to pray and directs us in what to pray for. That's what it means to pray in the Spirit (Jude 20).

So, we pray to the Father, in the name of Jesus, and with the help of the Holy Spirit.

Why does he instruct us to address God as, "Our father in heaven?"

There is a slight difference in the wording that Jesus used in this Matthew 6 passage and the passage in Luke 11, when he was talking to his disciples.

Most scholars believe that Jesus was speaking in Aramaic here, as with most if not all of his teaching. Aramaic was the common tongue of the Jewish world, though most also spoke Greek, being the universal language of international commerce. The Gospel authors would have translated Jesus' words into Greek, so that the Gentile world, who would not understand

Aramaic, would be able to understand Jesus' words. But in these two passages, there is a clue in the Greek and our English that indicates Jesus was using slightly different words for *father.*

In Matthew 6, he used the formal Aramaic word for father, that spoke of respect and reverence. In Luke 11, he used the informal word for father (Abba) that a small child would use to speak to his dad. It was more familiar and intimate.

This helps us understand the tension we can feel between the respect and reverence we are to have for our creator and master of the universe, and the intimacy that we can also enjoy with him as the one who loves us dearly, and is to us an earthly dad who cares for, protects, and looks out for our needs.

Jesus taught his followers to refer to God both ways. Our God is great and mighty, more awesome than we can imagine. All the power of the universe flows from and is contained within him. He is indeed magnificent and one to be feared. It is vital that we recognize this about him. We need to know who we are talking to. He is the creator of everything that is in existence.

And he is our loving father, who is good and kind and merciful, who cares about us, and knows us so well that even the hairs on our heads are counted.

He is a great God, and he is a good God. He is awesome, and he is loving.

That's who we are talking to when we pray, "Our father in heaven."

When we pray, who are we to pray to?

What does it mean for us to pray in Jesus' name?

How does the Holy Spirit help our praying?

Your Goal

*"Our Father in heaven, **hallowed be your name.** Your kingdom come, your will be done, on earth as it is in heaven. Give us this day our daily bread, and forgive us our debts, as we also have forgiven our debtors. And lead us not into tempta- tion, but deliver us from the evil one."*

This is kind of a theme of this chapter. Because of our sin nature, we can quickly slip into a selfish focus and allow our sin to infect our praying to the point where we are trying to be god and getting the real God to serve us, instead of the other way around. "Hallowed be your name," speaks di- rectly to this.

It doesn't help us in that most English translations use that word, "hallowed," which is not a word we are familiar with, outside of the Bible. Jesus had something specific in mind, but the English here is archaic.

An easier way for us to understand that phrase is this way, "May your name be revered as entirely unique and holy." It reveals a desire to see God truly honored as the Lord God in the world today.

The name of God speaks of God himself. To want God's name honored is to want God himself to be honored. It says, in effect, "You are the one and only God. May all the world know that." It points to the goal in this prayer to be for God's honor and glory, not our own satisfaction of imme- diate wants or desires.

Your Kingdom

*"Our Father in heaven, hallowed be your name. **Your kingdom come,** your will be done, on earth as it is in heaven. Give us this day our daily bread, and forgive us our debts, as we also have forgiven our debtors. And lead us not into temptation, but deliver us from the evil one."*

Few monarchies exist in our world today, so while we may understand Jesus' analogy of God's kingdom, we don't really identify with it the way his original listeners would have.

But for most of human history, almost all governments around the world were under the authority of a supreme monarch. Since God alone is the one and only supreme ruler of the universe, that everything came into existence by him and it all stays in existence by his direction, it's a fitting analogy and one that most people throughout history could embrace.

Jesus spoke of the kingdom of God often, and he was referring both to a future time when he will set things straight and reign here on the earth, but also of a spiritual kingdom that includes all those who have given themselves over to God's rule in their hearts and lives.

Jesus taught us to pray for God's kingdom to come. It was a reference to God's coming kingdom in the future. Seeing how bad things are in this world where God's rule is rejected and those in power are sinful and self-serving, we ought to have a longing for the day when Jesus is the literal king and this world is under his authority. We should pray for that.

But there is more to this request.

We are all busy building little kingdoms for ourselves. Our lives and everything in them, they are like little kingdoms. Your kingdom is your world, involving your family, your job or career, your habits and hobbies, friendships and daily activities. Everything that you control or have influence over is your kingdom.

This request Jesus asked us to pray is really about who's in charge. Who's the king? Are you going to be your own little king? Like Billy Joel sang, "I don't care what you say this is my life." Is that how you view your life? Or do you really want your kingdom to be part of God's kingdom, and for your rule and control to be submitted to his rule and control?

Who's in charge of your agenda? Who determines what you do? Where do you get your values from? How do you make your decisions? What is behind those choices? Are you the king of your own kingdom? Or maybe you've made someone else the king…your husband or wife, or worse yet, your kids.

Who's in charge of your world? Your life?

Is God?

So, do you really want HIS Kingdom to come?

Wanting God's kingdom to come means letting him lead today. If you want his kingdom to come, you'd let him be your king, king in your heart, king over your choices, king over your friendships, king over the way you use your time and your money.

That's why Jesus taught us to pray, "Your kingdom come." He wants you to say, "Your kingdom before mine. Invade my kingdom and take over. I want you in charge."

Will you pray that way?

Your Will

*"Our Father in heaven, hallowed be your name. Your kingdom come, **your will be done, on earth as it is in heaven**. Give us this day our daily bread, and forgive us our debts, as we also have forgiven our debtors. And lead us not into temptation, but deliver us from the evil one."*

C. S. Lewis wrote, "The moment you wake up each morning, all your wishes and hopes for the day rush at you like wild animals. And the first job each morning consists in shoving it all back; in listening to that other voice, taking that other point of view, letting that other, larger, stronger, quieter life come flowing in."

Lewis paints an accurate picture of my morning. And that's a big reason I need to pray early in the morning, every morning. Surrendering my will to Jesus, as I pray, is a very important foundation for my day.

That's essentially what Jesus was teaching in this next request. It is closely related to the last, and equally difficult, while also life-changing. Jesus was teaching us to ask the Father for his will to be done here on earth the same way his will is done in heaven.

Of course, God's will is done perfectly in heaven. There is no sin there, and all the angels and the natural world are in perfect harmony with God and his will. At God's home base, everything is according to his will. And that's why it's perfect.

But that's not always the case here on the earth. We know that a lot of things happen here that God is not in favor of. He is still absolutely sovereign and could step in and change things immediately, but for him to do that he would have to take away from us our free will, and turn us from moral creatures into biological robots. God wants us to desire his will and for our will to be conformed to his.

The fact that God's will is not always done on earth is also the reason for our problems. Rejecting God's will, in essence, is the nature of sin. And the problems around our world today are the results and aftermath of sin's corruption on mankind and the planet we inhabit. We have problems because we've rejected God's will.

If things are to be set straight on earth, God's will must be done on earth. Our will must be conformed to his.

But typically, in our praying, we are trying to accomplish the opposite. We are trying to get God's will to conform to ours. That's backwards, isn't it?

Jesus taught us to pray for God's will to be done on earth, perfectly, in the same way God's will is done in heaven.

It's one thing to pray that way when thinking of world events, national and international politics, world hunger, etc. It's another thing to pray that way when it comes to your own life.

Do you always want God's will to be done in your life? Do you want God's will when it comes to how you conduct yourself in your marriage, your job, with your friends, what you do in your free time? Can you honestly pray, "God, I want your will in my life. I want to do your will."?

This is how Jesus was teaching us to pray. This kind of praying involves surrendering our will to God. And it goes to the very heart of the definition of prayer...remember? An "exchange of wishes." Exchanging our will for God's will.

Look up James 4:1-3. What does James say is the cause of our fights and wars?

In verse 3, why does he say that we often pray for things but do not receive them?

Do you see a connection between these two? What is it?

Daily Bread

"Our Father in heaven, hallowed be your name. Your kingdom come, your will be done, on earth as it is in heaven. **Give us this day our daily bread,** *and forgive us our debts, as we also have forgiven our debtors. And lead us not into temptation, but deliver us from the evil one."*

Finally, it is time for the requests! Right? I mean, the way most of us pray, this is where we start. We go to God, maybe ask him to forgive us for

THE GOD PROJECT • 185

some things that are on our minds that we are feeling guilty about, and then head straight to the things that we want, mainly whatever desire we've been recently obsessed with. And that's why our prayers are shallow, and unanswered.

It's not that God doesn't want us to pray for our needs. But before we get to those things, we have to have our thinking reconfigured. Jesus taught us to do that by the way we pray. This is why Jesus brought this lesson.

So, he taught us to start by thinking about who we are talking to, "Our Father..." And then he taught us to pray for God's kingdom to invade ours, for us to let him take the reins, and to take charge of our lives. Then he taught us to sincerely submit to his will. Then...then...after we get those really important things taken care of, he wants us to bring our needs and desires to him. Once we have the right attitude towards those needs and desires, he's all ears.

Jesus told us to pray, "Give us this day our daily bread." No doubt, this is an abbreviation of all that we would ask for. Not only do we need food, we also need shelter, clothing, help with our relationships, guidance with our work, wisdom in raising our kids, etc. But Jesus said, "Give us *this day* our *daily* bread," for a reason. He wants us to pray daily, for the needs of that day. He wants us to depend on him every day, and the way we pray should reflect that.

In Exodus 16, there is a wonderful story of God's provision for his people, the children of Israel. They had recently escaped Egypt and were traveling through a wilderness area on their way to their forefathers' land which God had promised to give them. But on the way, they ran out of food. The Lord had Moses (who was their leader) gather them together to announce how we was going to provide for them. He told them that in the morning, they would find food scattered all over the ground. They were to go out and gather just enough for themselves and their families, but that they were not to hoard it. They were only to gather enough for that day.

The morning came and sure enough, all over the place where the Israelites were camped, there was a fluffy white bread-like substance, that had a bit of a honey taste to it. When the people came out of their tents and saw the food, they asked, "What is it?" Or, in their tongue, *"Manna?"*

So, the people gathered enough manna for the day. However, some disobeyed for fear of not having food in the future, and gathered more than what they needed for that day. In the morning, the leftover manna had a bad odor and was infested with worms. They learned that they were to look to God every day for their daily bread. And this was Jesus' reference in this prayer.

It's not that we should never pray for things in the future. But Jesus referred to the incident of manna for a reason. God wants us to come to him every day about *today* and to not be anxious about and wasting energy on the future.

If we pray for and trust God for today, and do that every day, tomorrow will take care of itself, because we will be praying for and trusting God for that day also, when it comes. But becoming concerned about the future before it's time erodes our trust in God and it soon turns into worry. So, Jesus instructed us to pray for our needs today, trusting God now. We'll have tomorrow to pray for and trust him for then.

It's during this time in my praying that I bring out my prayer list. My list includes my immediate and extended family, my coworkers, friends who have asked me to pray for them in specific ways, and my own requests. I believe in praying specifically. I bring the requests to God and share with him what I'd like to see happen. I acknowledge that my *wanter* is broken and I may be asking for things that are not best. I've already submitted my will to him, so it's natural now for me to ask him for his will in all the situations I am praying for.

I pray for people who have relationship issues, health problems, job needs, as well as those asking for wisdom or guidance. And I go through an actual written list. It helps me to stay focused and on track. It reminds me of things that my loved ones are going through and allows me to pray for them in specific ways. And in it all, I do my best to leave my request with God and trust him for how he answers.

It's also during this time that I spend a lot of time thanking God. Honestly, in my life, I have very few *real* needs. I have food and shelter, a good job, and lots of supportive people in my life. I have far more to thank God for than things I need to ask him for. And Paul wrote in Philippians 4:6, that the antidote for worrying is praying *with thanksgiving*. I take that literally. And I believe that praising and thanking God for his goodness is the way to build faith and to trust God for the future. When we pay attention to and verbalize our gratitude to God for his goodness, we become more confident in his care for the future.

Confess

> *"Our Father in heaven, hallowed be your name. Your kingdom come, your will be done, on earth as it is in heaven. Give us this day our daily bread, and **forgive us our debts**, as we also have forgiven our debtors. And lead us not into temptation, but deliver us from the evil one."*

Jesus also taught us to ask God for his forgiveness. God promises forgiveness for all of our sins, past, present, and future, based on Jesus' death on the cross. This was explained in chapter five. We would call this *positional forgiveness*. That Jesus took our sin and the father, based on Jesus' work, declared us to be righteous. That was the grand exchange of the cross and resurrection.

But there is another aspect of forgiveness that we need on a regular basis. We would call it *relational forgiveness*. Because we still sin, our daily relationship with God is interrupted, and each time we sin, we are in need of relational restoration.

A good example can be found in our human relationships. When I say something unkind to my wife, or ignore a request from her, or purposefully do something that I know would irritate her, it doesn't mean we are no longer married. But those sins against her hurt our relationship and create distance between us. Because I'm human and mess up all the time, it's important that I stay on top of those things and confess and seek her forgiveness when I do sin against her. And it's important that she do the same. It's how we've been able to grow closer together over the years and now, after being married for 33 years, our relationship is stronger than ever. But that means there had to be a lot of confessing and forgiving, which there

188 • SCOTT ZIEGLER

has been.

It's that way with friendships as well. For every human relationship to remain strong and growing, there must be confession on an ongoing basis. Genuine confession and forgiveness builds relationships when the participants are sinners. And we all are.

While God is not a sinner, he never sins against us, we are, and we sin against him all the time, even after becoming Christians. When we sin, we do not *lose our salvation.* But we do hinder the relationship. So, it's necessary for us to confess and receive his daily forgiveness.

Read 1 John 1:9. What does John promise that God will do?

What does he say we must do?

The Greek word in 1 John 1:9, *homologeow,* literally means to "say the same thing as" or "to agree." Actually, the root of our English word, confess, also means that (con- "with"/fess- "say"). To confess means to both admit what you did, and agree that it was wrong.

If you minimize what you did, or blame the other person, or even your circumstances, you are not really confessing. To genuinely confess something, you must take full responsibility for what you did, and agree with what God thinks about it. It's saying something like, "I did _____ and it was very wrong." Followed by, "Please forgive me."

Like praying for our daily bread, this underscores our need to pray every day, and throughout the day, because we sin regularly. We need to continually confess.

Remember John's promise here. God is gracious and eager to forgive. Some worry that they might forget about a sin. What then? Is the relationship still hindered? God is not sitting in heaven waiting for us to mess up so that he can resent us. He loves us and is gracious and is eager to forgive. Yes, we should confess our individual sins. But don't let this turn into a legalistic hardship that keeps you from enjoying him. He'll bring to your mind those areas to confess and to work on. But more than anything, he wants there to be honest dialog between you, with a heart of humility and a sincere desire to love him and follow him. Enjoy his grace and forgiveness!

Forgive

> *"Our Father in heaven, hallowed be your name. Your kingdom come, your will be done, on earth as it is in heaven. Give us this day our daily bread, and forgive us our debts,* **as we also have forgiven our debtors***. And lead us not into temptation, but deliver us from the evil one."*

I can't say all that needs to be said about our need to forgive others in this section or emphasize it enough. The heart and soul of Christianity is forgiveness. We have received God's forgiveness, and now God requires that we pass that forgiveness on to those who have wronged us.

Notice the terminology that Jesus uses. Instead of the word, "sin." Jesus uses the word, "debt." We ask God to forgive us our debts, and we are to forgive others their debts. There is a reason for this.

When we wrong another person, we take something from them. When someone wrongs us, they take something from us. It might be something tangible, like stealing an item of value. It might be something intangible, like reputation, innocence, or self-respect. So, when we've been wronged, we often become angry because we sense this inequity. "He owes me! What he did cost me my job!" Or, "I gave three years of my life to him. I invested a lot of time and energy into this relationship. And now he dumped me! He owes me!"

At the heart of the anger we feel towards those who have wronged us is a feeling of inequity. They took from us. They owe us. That's why we are angry.

And the only answer is forgiveness.

This mattered a lot to Jesus and he taught on it often.

Read Matthew 18:21-22. What was Peter's question for Jesus?

How did Jesus respond?

What do you think Jesus meant by his answer?

Read the story that Jesus tells right after this. What was the point of Jesus' story?

In the verses after Jesus' teaching on prayer in Matthew 6, the passage we have been studying, Jesus went on to say, "If you forgive those who sin against you, your heavenly Father will forgive you. But if you refuse to forgive others, your Father will not forgive your sins." (Matthew 6:14–15 NLT).

Jesus was referring to our relational forgiveness here. By allowing others' offenses against us to be barriers in our relationships with them, we also build a barrier between us and God. In order to get things right with God, we have to forgive others, and be right with them. In other words, our horizontal relationships affect our vertical relationship. And Jesus was teaching that if we've really been impacted by our vertical relationship, it will affect our horizontal relationships. If we've truly been forgiven, if we understand the depth of the sin that we are guilty of and what God did in canceling our debt, we cannot help but pass that forgiveness on, and practice it in our relationships.

So, as I am confessing my sin to God and asking him to forgive me, I'm taking inventory of my relationships and actively forgiving those that I may have been holding grudges against because of their wrongs against me.

Protect

*"Our Father in heaven, hallowed be your name. Your kingdom come, your will be done, on earth as it is in heaven. Give us this day our daily bread, and forgive us our debts, as we also have forgiven our debtors. And **lead us not into temptation, but deliver us from the evil one.**"*

Jesus concludes his model prayer by teaching his followers to pray for protection. But notice that the protection he taught us to pray for is protection from temptation and from the devil.

When we read the prayers of early Christians, even when facing horrible threats of persecution, they did not pray for physical protection. Not that it would be wrong to do so, but that was not their focus. They were more concerned about their spiritual condition.

In Acts 4, after being beaten and threatened for proclaiming Jesus, they gathered and prayed that God would give them boldness to continue to proclaim Jesus. The protection they wanted was protection from giving in to the influence of godless people, and doing the will of the evil one. They asked for courage to continue to do what was right.

That's the kind of protection we should be praying for. We should pray that God provides us strength in the face of temptation, that he would lead us away from it, and that we would follow him and do right. We should pray that we would not fall into the clutches of Satan and be led astray by him, and that God would deliver us from the evil one's treachery.

Summary

If we pray the way Jesus taught his followers to pray, we can personalize his model prayer, and use it as an outline or guide.

- Pray to the Father in Jesus' name, looking to the Holy Spirit to guide.
- Pray for God's name to be lifted up and honored through your requests.
- Ask God for his kingdom to come and take over your kingdom.
- Surrender your will to him and sincerely ask for his will to be done in your life.
- Pray for your daily needs, as well as the needs of your loved ones.
- Present to him your wants and desires and exchange them for his.
- Confess your sins and ask for forgiveness.
- Grant forgiveness to those who have wronged you.
- Pray for protection from temptation and the devil.

You can pray this way, and if you do, it will be a powerful thing in your life. You may be on the precipice of great things that are beyond your imagination if you put this into practice. But the only way you will accomplish this is by doing the first two principles that Jesus taught about prayer: 1) Set aside a time and 2) make a place for prayer.

If you haven't done so already, make that place for prayer today, and right now, schedule the time you will be committed to pray every day.

> *"Call to Me, and I will answer you, and show you great and mighty things, which you do not know." – Jeremiah 33:3 NKJV*

CHAPTER 10

Grow Your Faith

Just last week I was paddling a kayak on a slow-moving river. I was going upstream, planning to then paddle back down. While I was moving against the current, I came across a muskrat swimming along the bank, looking for a good spot to go ashore. So, I stopped paddling and watched quietly. Before I knew it, the kayak had not only stopped moving forward, it was now being carried back downstream. Because when you stop forward progress heading upstream on a river, you immediately begin to travel back down.

And I thought about a lot of Christians I've known over my thirty plus years of ministry. I've known many young Christians who have grown into mature believers with strong faith. Others seemed to make progress for a while, but eventually began to recede in their commitment and faith. As they stopped making progress, they started to regress.

Most things in life are that way. If you are not growing, you are declining. An old man said to me many years ago, "I'm still learning more every day, and I try to grow all the time. I figure if I'm not growing, I'm dying." And this man, who had already had three heart attacks and three bypass surgeries, went on to live many more years, long beyond what anyone thought he would. I think it was because he never stopped learning and growing.

I used to have a large bush in the corner of my back yard. It grew every year after we moved in. One spring I noticed that it was smaller than the year before. It had stopped growing. By the next spring, it was gone.

Like paddling up river, like a growing plant, like a human life, if you are not progressing, you are regressing, dying.

If your faith is not growing, it is diminishing. God wants your faith to grow.

What God is Looking for in You

When you think about it, the one thing that matters to God more than anything is your faith, your trust in him in all things at all times. It is the most important aspect of your Christian walk.

Look back into the Old Testament. What was it that created problems in our relationship with God in the first place? When Satan first appeared to Eve and tempted her to sin, he began by introducing doubt. He asked, "Has God indeed said…?" When she told him that if they were to eat of the fruit of the Tree of Knowledge of Good and Evil, that God told them they would die, Satan responded, "You will not really die." He went on to convince them that if they did eat of the fruit, instead of dying, as God said, they would become like God…or become gods, themselves. When she began to doubt God, and when Adam and Eve began to think that God was withholding good from them, when they lost trust in him, that's when they sinned.

The first sin was committed because of a lack of faith in God. And in fact, every time we sin, we are doing just that. Every time we sin we are demonstrating that we believe our way is better for us than God's way. We are acting on our lack of faith.

Read Romans 14:23. What does Paul call a lack of faith here?

Read Hebrews 11:6. What is the only way we can please God?

Faith is the bedrock of any relationship. You cannot have an intimate relationship with anyone without having a strong trust, a mutual faith. Show me a woman who does not trust her husband, or vice versa, and I will show you a poor marriage that is disappointing to both of them. Because trust, or faith, is necessary for any relationship to be strong.

And so it is with our relationship with God.

People were often impressed by Jesus, but Jesus wasn't really impressed by others. Just twice do the Gospels say that Jesus was amazed by anyone. The first was due to their lack of faith. Jesus was amazed how the people of his home town of Nazareth had such little faith.

"He was amazed at their lack of faith" (Mark 6:6 NIV).

The other time was positive. Jesus was impressed by the strength of faith of a Roman centurion.

"When Jesus heard this, he was amazed at him, and turning to the crowd following him, he said, 'I tell you, I have not found such great faith even in Israel'" (Luke 7:9 NIV).

Can you imagine that being said about you, that Jesus was impressed by you, because of your faith? As we read in Hebrews 11:6, the only thing that will impress him is our faith. Otherwise, it is impossible to please him.

All of us have an innate desire to impress others. Even those people who say they don't care what anyone thinks of them, down deep inside, they do. It's part of who we are. I wonder if it isn't a trait that God created within us to be fulfilled in him, that we can please him, yes, even impress him, with our faith.

198 • SCOTT ZIEGLER

More than anything else, God wants to see in us a strong and growing faith.

How faith grows

Whether or not your faith grows is partly up to you. Think of faith like a muscle. It has to be exercised. There is a training process for faith, and that's how it grows.

The theological term for this is "progressive sanctification." It's a term that refers to the process we go through to become more like Jesus (who had a perfect faith).

The Apostle Paul spoke of three aspects of our salvation: justification, sanctification, and glorification.

Justification is the moment we are saved, when God declares us to be righteous, based on Jesus' death and resurrection. We are justified by believing in Jesus. Justification is by faith.

Glorification is that moment we will be translated from this world into the next. It will either happen at our death, or when Jesus returns for us (which he promised he will do). Glorification, like justification, is instantaneous and we have nothing to do with it. Both justification and glorification are works of God and we cannot contribute to either.

Sanctification, however, is the time between justification and glorification. It is not instantaneous, like the other two, but a process. That's why it's called *progressive* sanctification.

It is also different from justification and glorification in that we participate or cooperate with God in the work of sanctification. It is the work of God, but God uses our efforts to make it happen. And it demands our participation. A number of passages say things like, "Make every effort..." which speak of our part in sanctification. We have to put forth the effort to exercise and work our faith to see it grow.

Read 1 Timothy 4:7. What does Paul tell Timothy he must do to become godly?

If you have access to a New King James Version (online), look up this verse in that version. The word used here is probably more accurate to the original Greek. What is it?

What does that tell us about the process of growing our faith (becoming godly)?

The Enemy of our Faith (Spiritual Warfare)

But there is an enemy. Just as there is a real God, there is also a real devil. From the early pages of Genesis in the Bible, we read of this adversary who hates God and will do anything to attack him by hindering his beloved people from connecting with him. So, he goes after our faith.

We already saw this a couple of pages ago when talking about his attack on God's integrity with Eve in the Garden of Eden. In essence, he created a separation between people and God by disrupting their faith.

While your faith in God has now been revived, Satan has not given up on you. He will do all he can to hinder your growth, and tempt you to lose trust in God, because he knows that will be the most hurtful thing he can do to God.

Read 1 Peter 5:8. What two words or names does Peter use to describe Satan and what do these words mean?

What analogy does he use of the devil? He is like a what? And how does he further this warning?

What does this tell you about the threat of this enemy?

So, the threat of the evil one (see Jesus' reference in John 17:15) is very real. He will do all he can to attack and destroy your faith and create distance in your heart from God.

However, God has not left us without a strong defense. From the Bible, we can know what Satan's strategy is and how we can defeat him with God's power.

Satan has no authority over you. He cannot control you or make you do anything. His tools are deceit, division, and temptation. Besides those things, he cannot do anything to you.

The evil one deceives by casting doubt on God's goodness. He tempts us into thinking that sin will be beneficial for us. Our lack of trust then leads us to believe that things God told us are harmful, are good. And when we fall prey to that deceit and doubt, we give in to temptation and do the things that bring about guilt and pain, taking us further away from our trust in God.

Read Ephesians 6:10-18. Who is at war with us?

Where does our strength against this evil one come from?

What does the Apostle Paul tell us to do, in order to be protected from and defeat Satan?

What are the defensive weapons that Paul speaks of?

What is the only offensive weapon, and why would that be?

In some Christian circles, believers become enamored with the concept of spiritual warfare, and use religious formulas and rituals to cast out demons, often sensationalizing it. Attempting to do battle this way then becomes mysterious and intriguing. But we should be careful about this. We have a God who is sovereign and while there is a whole spiritual world in existence beyond our senses that we do not understand, it is not beyond God's understanding or control.

C.S. Lewis said, "There are two equal and opposite errors into which our race can fall about the devils. One is to disbelieve in their existence. The other is to believe, and to feel an excessive and unhealthy interest in them."

The Apostle Paul's answer to the threat of Satan was not in repeating special formulas, or "binding Satan" (something we cannot do), but in putting on the armor of God (Ephesians 6:10-18) and using His power to protect you.

Go back to 1 Peter 5:8, only this time, look at the next verse, v. 9. What does Peter say we should do in response to the threat of the devil?

Now read James 4:7. How does Jesus' half-brother tell us to defeat Satan?

So, real spiritual warfare involves strengthening ourselves with God's presence (protected with his armor), submitting ourselves to God, standing firm in our faith (or our trust in God), disbelieving the devil's lies and re-sisting his temptations, and growing our faith in God as we follow him in every way.

The Process of Growth

Just as the devil will do everything he can to hinder our spiritual growth, we defeat him by growing spiritually, or growing in our faith.

By looking at the process of the spiritual growth of key Bible characters such as the Apostle Paul, as well as how people grow in faith by observation and their own testimony, we can see that five ingredients or catalysts seem to work together to produce a growing faith. By taking advantage of these things that God makes available to us, we can see our faith grow and our Christian walk become spiritually mature.

To continue to grow in your faith, it is very important that you involve yourself in these five areas. Do everything you can to manage your schedule and your life to allow these catalysts to bind together with other elements God has brought into your life for you to become more like Jesus and closer in your relationship with him.

(These next five catalysts are seen in Acts 9 in the growth process of the Apostle Paul, but the terms themselves are borrowed from Andy Stanley in his book, *Deep and Wide*.)

Providential relationships

Before Acts 9, Saul was the chief persecutor of Jesus' church. After Acts 9, Saul was the chief promoter of Jesus' church. It's hard to imagine anyone growing more rapidly than he did early in his Christian life.

It all started with relationships that God gave him immediately after his conversion, relationships with other believers who challenged and facilitated his growth. These new Christian friends inspired him and supported him. They protected him and challenged him.

That's what the right kinds of friends will do for us. One of the most important things we can do in our lives to help us grow spiritually, is to surround ourselves with people who will help us grow in our relationship with God.

Life change of any kind is most often fueled by relationships.

Read Proverbs 13:20. What does Solomon say happens to you if you hang out with wise people?

What is the flip side of this? What happens to those who hang with the wrong people (fools)?

Every relationship you have either bolsters your faith, or detracts from your faith. This principle will work behind the scenes every day in your life.

Honestly, though, the most dangerous relationships are not anti-church or anti-god people. I try to keep at least a couple of them in my life because they wind up challenging me, and are also great outlets for witnessing.

Instead, I think the most dangerous relationships are friendships with professing Christians who are complacent. Those who say they have faith in God, but it doesn't seem to matter to them. Their faith isn't changing them. And we watch them and we think, "Why am I investing into my faith and resisting temptation, and maintaining a prayer life, and blocking time out for God and serving in his church when that friend is doing none of that and he seems fine."

Those relationships have proven to be the most destructive, in my experience.

I've heard it said, "The best you can hope to be is the average of the five people you're around the most." That kind of makes you think twice about who those five people are!

If you have lazy friends. You'll tend to be lazy.

If you have industrious and successful friends–chances are they'll rub off on you.

If you have friends who are always in the middle of drama, you'll have a drama filled life (and I don't mean that as a good thing).

If you hang out with good husbands and fathers, they will grow on you (*whoever walks with the wise will become wise*). But if you hang out with women who are dissing their men, you'll probably become a husband critic too.

It's not that you can walk around your church lobby between services and ask people who appear to be good Christians to be your friends. That would just be weird. But you can put yourself in an atmosphere that is conducive to meeting the right kinds of friends, and then pursuing those friendships in a way that does not scare them off.

Be faithful to attending church weekly and engage in simple conversations with those sitting near you. Who knows what that may eventually lead to. Get involved in a community group and/or attend a study group. Seek to get together with a few in that group outside of church or group time. Join a ministry team and serve. Serving alongside others is a great way to get to know other people.

I made lifelong friends who made a major difference in my early Christian walk at church, in Bible studies and while serving on ministry teams. These were the kinds of friends who helped my faith grow.

Practical teaching

There is something about hearing and applying the teaching of God's Word that produces giant steps of spiritual growth in our lives. Paul heard the teaching of God's Word shortly after his conversion and it fueled his growth.

Personally, I can point to three or four sermons that I heard early in my Christian life that propelled me forward on my spiritual journey. I think most mature Christians can look back on their journey and quickly point to a few sermons that changed them.

Perhaps even more than that, it was *regularly listening* to practical sermons that produced lots of growth in our early Christian walk and gave us a foundation for later growth.

But there is an important element in this that can't be ignored. Just hearing is not enough. You have to do something with what you hear. You have to put it into practice for it to make a difference and produce spiritual growth.

Read Romans 10:17. How does faith come?

Read Matthew 7:24-29. This was at the closing of Jesus's famous "Sermon on the Mount." To what does Jesus compare those listeners who both hear and practice his teaching?

What does he say about those who hear it, but do not put it into practice?

So, Jesus emphasized the importance of listening to and putting into practice the teaching of God's Word. It's important that we *hear* good Bible teaching, and that we *practice* what we hear.

There are some ways we can make sure to do this.

First, be faithful to church and listen carefully to every sermon. (I don't say that because I'm a Bible teacher. I'm a Bible teacher because I believe it is so important!).

When you miss a week at church, get caught up by listening online. Remember, most sermons are part of a series, and each one fits with the rest in a cohesive way. By missing one sermon, it's like skipping a chapter of a book. The rest of the series will not be nearly as impactful if you are skipping some of the sermons. So, stay caught up.

We can also seek out other ways to hear the teaching of God's Word and supplement what we are getting in church. Our church, like most churches, offers multiple opportunities to take additional study classes to learn more Bible. Sign up for those classes and attend them consistently. There are also a lot of great teaching resources online. What a great way to redeem your commute to and from work or school, by listening to podcasts of practical Bible teaching. (Contact one of your pastors to get suggestions on who to listen to.)

But once again, it's not enough to just hear the teaching. For it to help us grow, we must *do it*. After every sermon, ask yourself, "What did I learn?" and, "What should I do?"

Personal ministry

There's something about serving that makes us more like Jesus. After all, Jesus was the epitome of service. Though he was God, he came to earth to be a servant. If we want to grow to become like him (which is what sanctification is all about), we will have to learn to serve.

Read Matthew 14:13-33. What in the text tell us that Jesus probably didn't feel like doing things with other people when the passage opens?

The disciples were also tired and hungry. But in this passage, what did Jesus instruct them to do?

What part did they play in seeing this miracle take place?

What did they get to do after everyone was fed, and what was that miracle?

Now briefly read the story that follows, starting in verse 22. It also involves a famous miracle; this time with Peter, the Apostle. What great feat did he accomplish and what does that say about how his part in feeding the 5,000 affected his faith, and his willingness to get out of the boat?

Getting involved in serving others in the context of Jesus' church is what we call "ministry." And at our church, we believe that everyone should have a ministry. Not because the church needs it (though it would be impossible for any church to operate effectively without lots of people serving), but because it grows our faith.

After Saul's conversion in Acts 9, he immediately began to stretch and exercise his new faith by serving (v. 20). And he did it in ways that demanded his faith to grow.

Taking on the responsibility of a personal ministry does wonders for our walk of faith. And for some, it is the main catalyst for growth. I've known mature believers who point back to teaching a kids' Bible lesson that got them into the Bible for the first time, just to prepare their lesson. Others have talked about the impact of serving with other men in a parking lot ministry and how those conversations and simple acts of service for others gave them a sense of ownership in the church and helped them grow spiritually. It also brought them to church on days when they would have been tempted to skip, adding the additional elements of being around *providential relationships* and hearing *practical teaching* on a more consistent basis.

So, if you haven't yet, find a place to serve at church. You could become a greeter, help give groceries to needy families, work in kids' ministry, or hand out bulletins. God is doing great things. He wants you to help divide the food and enjoy the full baskets after the miracle!

Private disciplines

Another catalyst for spiritual growth is private disciplines. Sometimes we call these *spiritual disciplines*, because they involve spiritual activity that require discipline to maintain consistently. And it's in the nature of that consistency, and in fact, being hard to maintain, that actually produces the growth.

If something isn't hard, it probably doesn't do us a lot of good.

Look up 1 Timothy 4:7. What word is used that reminds us that spiritual growth takes some work?

For most people, seeing the word, "discipline," doesn't make us all that excited about reading this section. But just about everything in life that is worthwhile takes discipline. You've heard the saying, "If it were easy, everyone would be doing it."

As we said earlier, growing your faith is like growing a muscle. It takes work, effort, and some discomfort to make a muscle grow. That's also how spiritual growth works. We grow by stretching and stressing our faith, putting effort into spending time with God and learning his word, and doing hard things that he asks us to do.

Disciplines do start out hard. But after a while, they actually become something we look forward to, even fun. After the habit is established, what once was a chore, becomes a beneficial lifestyle.

When I began running, it was a chore just to put on my running shoes. I hated it. My initial goal was to just make it a single block. I couldn't imagine running an entire mile without walking. But seven months later, I completed my first marathon.

It started out hard. But after a while I began to look forward to runs. When I was traveling and could not get my run in, it bothered me and I couldn't wait to get back to my routine.

That is the nature of discipline. You have to get through the initial stages of doing what is hard until it turns into a habit, and then a lifestyle.

Something else to remember, discipline always results in progress, even if you have a bad attitude about it. When I began running, even though I did not want to, I was making progress in my breathing, my heart rate, my weight loss, and my muscle tone. Having a good attitude makes the chore easier to accomplish, but accomplishing it is just as beneficial if you don't.

I've learned to do the discipline no matter how I feel and the discipline itself eventually brings my attitude around.

In his famous "Sermon on the Mount," Jesus talked about practicing spiritual disciplines in private, and how doing so brings about the greatest reward. This is why we call them, "Private Disciplines."

Read Matthew 6:1-16. What three "disciplines" does Jesus talk about in this passage?

What is his point in verse 1?

He follows this instruction up with what three examples of spiritual disciplines?

Where does Jesus say we should go we pray? And why would that be?

The kind of private disciplines that will grow our faith involve spending time alone with God, such as prayer & fasting, and reading & studying God's word. It takes discipline to do this on a daily basis, but it is also spiritually rewarding. It's like a spiritual workout. It strengthens our faith.

But Jesus also mentions giving as a spiritual discipline that should be done in private. How is it that these acts, being done in private, would grow our faith?

Pivotal circumstances

The fifth catalyst for spiritual growth involves things that happen to us that we cannot control. But how we respond to the circumstance determines whether or not we grow.

Many mature Christians of strong faith point to a make or break event in their lives that became the single most important catalyst for their spiritual growth. They talk about the choices they made in that experience and how that shaped their future walk of faith. It could be a job loss, health crisis, or broken relationship. How we respond and whether or not we trust and obey God in the middle of that critical moment will make a major difference in our walk of faith.

We call these circumstances 'pivotal' because when they happen, we can move towards or away from God. When facing a difficult situation, we can blame God or trust God. That choice will determine, in the long run, whether faith will grow or diminish.

When you think about it, in every hero or villain tale or movie, the main character is shaped by a pivotal circumstance. Batman lost his parents. Spiderman was raised by his uncle who was tragically killed. Iron Man was kidnapped by terrorists. The protagonist in Alfred Hitchcock's, *Psycho* lost his mom. In *Hunger Games*, Katniss' father died and her mother went emotionally AWOL. These were pivotal circumstances that shaped the characters, based on their response to those situations. Their approach to life was largely formed by their response to their difficult situations. Some responded well, some poorly. The circumstances were pivotal.

Sometimes a pivotal circumstance may be a good experience, but usually, it's a major trial of some sort. In his book, *The Problem of Pain*, C.S. Lewis wrote: "God whispers to us in our pleasures, speaks in our conscience, but shouts in our pains: it is His megaphone to rouse a deaf world."

Read James 1:2-4. What does James (Jesus' half-brother) say that trials can do for us?

James refers to these trials as "testing of your faith." It is also a "stressing" of our faith. If we respond by moving toward God, the circumstance, no matter how difficult, will help our faith grow. But if we move away from God in response to it, no matter how good a thing it might be, it will erode our faith. The key lies in our response. Will we allow this to bring us closer to God and to trust him more, or will we turn away from him and instead rely on ourselves?

Sometimes God allows these things to come into our lives. But sometimes, he even causes them. In John 11, we have the story of Jesus' friend, Lazarus, who had become ill, and then died. Jesus was alerted when his friend first became sick, in hopes that Jesus would go and heal him. But in the story, Jesus purposely stayed where he was and allowed Lazarus to die. He could have healed him and kept him from dying, but he didn't. In v. 15, he tells his disciples that he did not go immediately so that their faith would grow.

This was a pivotal circumstance that Jesus intentionally put his disciples and his friends Mary and Martha through. And he waited to see if they would respond in faith, or in anger. In the end, Jesus raised Lazarus from the dead, which, in and of itself, was an amazing miracle, of course! But there was another lesson in this story. It was a story of stress that Jesus put his disciples and friends through in order to grow their faith. And at the close of this story (v. 45) we read that many who witnessed these events believed in Jesus (the word used for believe is the word for "faith"), while others went and reported it to the Pharisees who then sought to get rid of him.

It was a pivotal circumstance that Jesus intentionally put people through. Some responded with an increase of faith and turned toward him. Others responded by rejecting him.

And that's the choice we have with every stressful situation we are placed in. It could be the loss of a job or the death of a loved one. It could be news of a health concern or a major relationship struggle. In my life, I was made homeless early in my Christian life at the age of 17.

If you are not in the middle of a pivotal circumstance, there is probably one coming. You get ready for the big stuff by responding well to the little stuff. Decide now how you will respond to these pivotal circumstances, and practice responding for the big things by responding well to the smaller things.

How do you respond well to pivotal circumstances? By taking refuge in the other mechanisms for growing your faith that we studied in the last few pages: biblical teaching, providential relationships, private disciplines, and personal ministry.

Though you may be going through a trial, stay faithful in attending church and listening carefully to and applying the sermons. Get around people who will be good for you and will encourage you in your faith. Get alone with God to talk with him and read his Word every day. And serve others in the context of the church. Doing for others will in the long run be beneficial to you.

By sticking with these mechanisms for growing our faith during difficult times or pivotal circumstances, we will come out the other side much stronger and with greater faith.

What is the one thing that God wants to see happen in you?

What is the theological term used in the Bible for growing our faith?

Satan will oppose our growth of faith. How will he attempt to do this?

How are we to protect ourselves from his attack?

What are the mechanisms that God uses to grow our faith?

CHAPTER 11

Give Back

The epic movie, *Saving Private Ryan*, concludes with a moving scene. This very realistic war drama, set in World War 2, depicted a small company of Army Rangers on a mission to safely bring back Private James Ryan, since his three other brothers had all been lost in the war. During the film, several of the Ranger squad lost their lives in the mission to bring Ryan home. In a moving scene toward the end of the movie, the squad leader's last words to Private Ryan were, "James ... earn this. Earn it!"

The movie closes in present times (present when the movie was made –late 90s) with the elderly Private Ryan revisiting Captain Miller's grave. He looks up at his wife and asks her to confirm that he had led a good life, that he is a 'good man' and thus worthy of the sacrifice of Miller and the others. It is evident that he lived his entire life attempting to be worthy of the sacrifices that were made for him.

In truth, we could live a thousand lives working to make ourselves worthy of Jesus' sacrifice, but we could never do it. Jesus himself simply decided that our salvation was a worthwhile cause for him. So, he gave his life for us.

We could never make ourselves worthy. But we can respond in gratitude. We can do what he asked us to do with our lives in return. We can give back.

In the last chapter, we talked about growing our faith and our relationship with God. The natural outcome of this growth will be a life of giving back to the God who rescued us. Jesus has asked us to follow his example and that example was all about serving his Father and loving other people.

Jesus taught that the two greatest commandments were to love God and love people (Matthew 22:38-39). He spent his life serving others and he taught his disciples that they were to follow this example (John 13:15).

When you consider all that God has done for you, saving you, forgiving you, preparing and reserving heaven for you, it should be a natural response to want to give back.

Read Psalm 24:1. Who owns everything?

What is the point of the Psalmist's question in Psalm 116:12?

What does David acknowledge in Psalm 31:15?

Read 1 Chronicles 29:13-14. When we give to God of our time, our abilities, or our money, where did it come from in the first place?

What was Paul's point in 2 Corinthians 8:9?

Read 2 Corinthians 9. What is Paul talking to the Corinthians about in this chapter?

Why do you think he closed off this chapter (and topic) the way he did?

Give Back from What We have Received

When my kids were little, at Christmas time they wanted to give my wife, Linda, and me gifts, but they had no money and no way to go shopping. Linda and I would take them shopping for each other's birthdays and Christmas, and of course, they would buy gifts for us from money that already belonged to us. So, in a sense, we were buying ourselves gifts. I especially used to get a kick out of how they would go around the house and find things that they knew we liked, and wrap them up and put them under the Christmas tree for us to open. But again, they were just giving us what we already owned. Linda and I both loved it, and cherished those gifts!

You read 1 Chronicles 29:13-14. That is exactly what David was saying. The gifts we give back to God already belong to him. We are giving back to him what he entrusted with us to manage. And yet, he loves it when we give to him what he already owns.

The three areas in particular that we should consciously give back to him are our time, our talents, and our treasures. All three came from him and belong to him. But as his trusted managers, he has asked us to give a portion of all three back to him. This is how we worship him with our lives.

Time

Not only is time the greatest gift you can give someone you love, when you think about it, it is the only gift you can give. Even when you give someone cash, or if you spend that same cash to buy something for them, your gift is the time it took for you to earn that money, and shop for the item. Time is our most valuable commodity.

Are you giving back to God of the time that he has given you?

Read Proverbs 27:1. What does this tell us about the time we have left in our lives?

What should that tell us about the value of time?

Read Ephesians 5:15-16. What does the Apostle Paul say here about how we should approach our time?

We tend to waste whatever we think we have excess of. We are careful to guard and protect what we believe is limited. Because we don't know how much time we have left in our lives, most of us think of it as being unlimited, like there will always be time to do things that are important to us. Often, we wind up procrastinating and wasting opportunities to do the things we know are more important, but were not prioritized because time was not important enough to us.

An incident from the American Revolution illustrates what tragedy can result from procrastination. Colonel Rahl was the commander of the British troops at Trenton, New Jersey, at the time Washington made his famous crossing of the Delaware. He was playing cards when a courier brought an urgent message informing him that General George Washington was making the crossing at that very moment. But Rahl put the letter in his pocket and didn't bother to read it until the game finished. When he finally opened and read the message, realizing the seriousness of the situation, he rushed to rally his men to meet the coming attack, but his procrastination made it too late. He along with many of his men were killed that night, and the rest of the regiment were captured.

Only when we understand the limited nature of our time and the few opportunities we have of doing the most important things, do we begin to accomplish those things that matter most.

When I'm speaking on this subject, I like to borrow an illustration from Steven Covey *(First Things First)*. Using two big buckets, large boulders, small rocks, and sand, I explain how the buckets represent our lives. The boulders represent the things we need to do that are most important. The rocks represent secondary priorities, but important things nonetheless. The sand represents doing things that don't really matter (television watching, etc.) but ways we still use our time.

In the first bucket, I pour the sand in first, and then all the smaller rocks. Then I try to put the boulders in the bucket, but they never fit.

In the second bucket, I first put in the boulders. I then pour the rocks in, which flow in and around the spaces between the boulders. Finally, I pour all the sand in, which fills in the rest of the space, even space between the smaller rocks.

In the first bucket, you can't fit it all in, because the sand and rocks take up valuable space. But in the second bucket, it all fits with quite a bit of room to spare. Because when you do those things that are most important first, you will always have time for the other things. But if you do those things of lesser importance first, you'll never get your priorities accomplished. And you'll be heard saying things like, "There's never enough time."

But there is enough time. You have time to do those things that matter most to you. God will always give us enough time to do the things he wants us to do. So, we need to figure out what the priorities are and do those things first.

Is giving back to God enough of a priority to you for him to be a boulder? Or do you treat him like sand? Is he highest on your list of priorities? Or does he only get leftover time, which often is not there after everything else comes first?

Read Matthew 16:25-27. The words "life" and "soul" are both used in this one passage, as though they were different concepts. But that would not have been Jesus' intent. He used the Greek word "psuche" in both places and the English translators made it "life" in one place and "soul" in the other. The word can be translated "breath, life, or soul" but in context, it is used to speak of our lives, or the time we live on earth. Read it again, this time substituting "time" for each occurrence of "soul" or "life."

How does that change your understanding of Jesus' words?

Here is what Warren Wiersbe said regarding this passage:

"Discipleship is a matter of profit and loss, a question of whether we will waste our lives or invest our lives. Note the severe warning Jesus gives us here: once we have spent our lives, we cannot buy them back! Remember, he was instructing his disciples, men who had already confessed him as the Son of God. He was not telling them how to be saved and go to heaven, but how to save their lives and make the most of the opportunities on earth. 'Losing your soul' is the equivalent of wasting your life, missing the great opportunities God gives you to make your life count. You may 'gain the whole world' and be a success in the eyes of men, and yet have nothing to show for your life when you stand before God. If that happens, though you did own the whole world, it would not be a sufficient price to give God to buy another chance at life."

So then…what is the most important use of the time God has given you in your life?

What are some ways that God wants us to give back our time?

How does daily quiet time fit into this?

How does corporate worship in church fit into this?

How does volunteer ministry fit into this?

How can we make giving our time back to God a priority?

Talents

Napoleon once pointed to a map of China and said, "There lies a sleeping giant. If it ever wakes up, it will be unstoppable."

That is exactly how I feel about the talents and abilities contained worldwide in the church.

A Gallup poll several years ago revealed that in American churches, only 10% of the members had an active role in church ministry. There is something sadly wrong with that.

Read Ephesians 4:11-12? Why were church leaders given to the church? What is their function?

Who are "the saints" that Paul is talking about?

So then, according to this passage, who is supposed to *do the work* of the ministry?

According to this passage, when leaders are equipping church members, and church members are actively volunteering (doing the work of ministry), what happens?

Read 1 Peter 4:10. What does Peter say about using our gifts and abilities to serve?

Read 1 Corinthians 12:4-7. What two things does Paul say there are a variety of?

But he says there is "one" Lord. And what is the "one" purpose for these gifts and ministries?

Now read vv. 12-27. Are any places of ministry or gifts more important than others?

With that passage in mind, what happens in the body, as well as in the church, when one member does not "show up" or use their abilities for ministry as we are all instructed?

No doubt, God has given you unique gifts, abilities, passions and experiences, that can be used for his kingdom work in the church. It may take a while for you to find what is the "perfect fit" for you, but the best way to find that fit is to look for the greatest need for volunteers in the church and plug your gifts, abilities, passions and experiences into filling that need. Over time, God will direct you to just the right place. But that direction only comes once we begin to obey him by answering his call to ministry involvement.

If you have not yet, find a place where you can plug into serving, commit yourself to doing it and be faithful, pouring yourself into it.

You might be surprised by the number of connections you will make with other people, and the personal fulfillment you will gain by giving back from the talents God has given you.

Treasure

These next several pages may contain the greatest potential for your spiritual growth than anything written in the last few chapters. I don't know what it is when it comes to our stuff, our money or the things that we can buy with it, but most of us sense real conflict with our material treasure and our spiritual lives. I've seen this conflict many times in new and growing Christians, that when they release the material things in their lives to God's control, a work of faith takes place within them that catapults their spiritual growth.

Consider this. There are about 500 verses in the Bible that talk directly about prayer. And I think we would all agree that prayer is a very important thing when it comes to our spiritual lives, right?

There are about 500 verses in the Bible that talk about faith. And as we saw in the last chapter, the number one thing that God wants to do in our lives is to build our faith. So, faith is a very important thing when it comes to our spiritual lives, right? Of course.

So…500 verses on prayer in the Bible; 500 verses on faith in the Bible. Guess how many verses there are in the Bible that talk about how we handle our money, and whether or not we are generous?

Can you guess? 500? Do you think there would be as many verses in the Bible about giving as there are verses on prayer or faith?

There are not 500 verses in the Bible that talk about money. No.

There are over 2,300 verses in the Bible that talk about how we handle our money! Two thousand three hundred! That's over four times the number of verses in the Bible that talk about prayer, and over four times the number of verses in the Bible that talk about faith!

Jesus, himself, talked about money a lot. He talked more about money, our attitude towards it, how we handle it, and how generous we are, than he did about heaven, hell, prayer, faith, and even love! Jesus talked more about money than any of these things. And not just a little bit more, a lot more.

In fact, of Jesus' 38 parables, 16 of them were about money. That's almost half!

So why is there so much in the Bible about money, how we handle it, and how generous we are with it? Why did Jesus talk about it so much?

Because the number one competitor that God has for our hearts is money. Jesus knew that. So, Jesus addressed.

Think about it. When was the last time you wondered, "Hmmm, should I serve God or the Devil? God or Satan? Which?"

You probably never thought that way even before you started this study, or before you gave your life to following Jesus. Even the Devil knows that he's not going to *directly* get your heart. He knows that he has to do it *indirectly.* And he does it pretty well with a lot of people through money, or the things that money can buy.

Even as followers of Jesus, we often go through an internal struggle over whether or not our hearts belong to God or to the things God gives us. We probably never say that out loud, but if we are being honest, we know the pull that things have on us. It can either be the quest for security in a bank account, or the status and pleasure of having things. But we all have to admit that money or the things that it can buy competes with God in our hearts.

It's true. We know it's true. God knows it's true. So, he talked about it, a lot.

Here's his solution: *1) be grateful* for what we have, and *2) be generous* with what he gives us.

Instead of setting our hearts on things we have or want, we are to set our hearts on the God who provides for us. Instead of finding our security and pleasure in things, we are to find our security and pleasure in the God who gives things to us, and does so generously.

We do that by regularly expressing gratitude (out loud and to others) and by generously giving back to God for his work, and to those in need.

When we do these two things, something happens in our hearts that produces joy and fulfillment that never takes place in our pursuit of money or things. We think that by getting more we will be happy, but the more we get, the more we want.

However, when we regularly express gratitude to God for his goodness, and generously give of what he has provided, that joy and fulfillment we seek comes as a by-product of our gratitude and generosity.

And here's something that you will learn by practicing these two vital principles, the two concepts are inextricably linked. You cannot be truly grateful without becoming generous. If you are truly grateful, you will automatically want to give. And by becoming generous, you also become grateful. Gratitude leads to generosity. But if you find yourself struggling with gratitude, by being generous anyway, you become more grateful. I don't know how it happens, but it works. When ungrateful people give, they become grateful. It just happens.

This section is not so much about gratitude, though. It's about giving. But I wanted you to see how giving helps produce gratitude. I sometimes hear people talk about how we should only give with the right attitude. And I get that. We should have the right attitude. But sometimes my attitude isn't right. I should still give even if it isn't. And what happens is…when I give anyway, my attitude changes. The act of giving does something in my heart to change my attitude.

It's like the time I went to the doctor several years ago. I had not been working out, and the doctor told me that my resting heart rate was too fast. He seemed concerned. I asked him how it could be fixed. And he literally wrote on a prescription sheet, "Work-out 30 mins. daily."

I looked up at him and said, "I can't work out if my heart isn't good." He laughed and said, "You have to start working out in order to get your heart working good."

And that's how it is with generosity. The only way to combat the ever-encroaching competition that money and things have on our hearts, is by practicing generosity, whether or not we feel like it.

Look up the following verses and summarize them.

Deuteronomy 8:17-18

Proverbs 3:9-10

Luke 6:38

Leviticus 27:30

Malachi 3:9-10

These last two verses talk about giving a "tithe." You may have heard of the concept before. The tithe was a tenth, or 10% of an Israelite's income that they were required to give back to God, under the Law of Moses. We are no longer bound by the Mosaic Law, as the Israelites were before Jesus. However, there are many good principles to learn and practice that are found in the Law.

In the New Testament, the tithe is not stipulated as a requirement for Christians. But the concept of giving based on percentage of income is. And something that Jesus taught is very important for us to remember. When he taught on the Law (Matthew 5-7), he taught his followers to exceed the expectations of the Law. So, the principle of tithing should not be ignored by us today. And there are some important New Testament Scriptures that help.

Read 1 Corinthians 16:2. Paul was talking about local church giving here. What day of the week did he say collections should be made, and why do you think on that day?

How much does he say each person should give?

Read Mark 12:41-44. How much did the rich people give?

How much did the widow give?

Based on this, does God care more about what dollar amount we give, or what percentage we give?

So, in the New Testament, while we are not required to tithe because of the Mosaic Law, we learn an important principle in that law that the New Testament does emphasize: giving by percentage. Our giving is viewed as generous from God's perspective, not by the dollar amount that we give, but by the percentage of our income that we give.

Read 2 Corinthians 8:1-8. List out everything you learn about giving from this passage.

Now read 1 Timothy 6:17-19. Do the same from this passage.

You probably don't think of yourself as rich. Few people do. Everybody seems to know someone who is rich, but few of them admit that they are rich. In fact, Gallup did a survey some years ago that revealed most Americans thought rich was a person who made about twice their annual income. So, people who make $50,000 a year think that rich is making $100,000 a year. People who make $100k think rich is someone who makes $200k. This keeps going up. In a *Money Magazine* survey, their subscribers, whose average net worth is $2.5 million, said that rich is someone who has $5 million in net worth. So, no matter how much we make, we think of a rich person as someone who makes twice what we make or has twice as much as we have.

But you are probably a lot richer than you care to admit. In fact, anyone who makes $45k/year in annual income has the buying power and lifestyle of the top 1% of the world. Maybe you haven't gotten there yet, but you probably will. And even if you are not in that top 1%, rich people in the first century would have traded all that they had to have what you enjoy. From their perspective, you would be fabulously rich!

I say all this so that you don't read through these verses and think that it isn't for you. It probably is. And even if you are not rich, by practicing these principles now, you'll be ready to properly handle any riches that may come in your future.

In this passage, Paul helps us to understand a key ingredient from keeping our hope in God from migrating to hoping in, trusting in, or finding fulfillment and pleasure in things, rather than in God who provides those things. He tells Timothy to remind rich people (that's us) to do more good, and to be more generous. As rich people, we are supposed to be more generous than other people.

Then in v. 19 he refers to something that Jesus taught often. Do you see it? He says that by being more generous we are able to store treasure for ourselves in heaven. Jesus taught that very thing a number of times. It's an amazing concept, that by being generous in this life, we are actually storing up treasure in heaven.

Remember this, the more we get, the more we want. But the more we give, the more we have in eternity, and in reality, the more we are able to enjoy what we have in this life as well.

Jesus was right. It *is* better to give than to receive (Acts 20:35).

So then, how much should we give? There are three principles from the New Testament that are important and help us here. We call them the three Ps of giving: *priority, percentage, progressive.*

Priority

We must make giving a priority. Since giving is an act of worship, and a way to recognize God as having first place in our lives, it should be the first thing we do with what we are entrusted with, our income. My wife and I have all of our giving at the top of our budget sheet, and we give first from our income. A big part of making giving a priority (see Proverbs 3:9), is predetermining how much it is going to be.

Most people never really become generous, even though they think they are, but they never really become generous in God's eyes, because their giving isn't enough of a priority to them to predetermine how much they will give. Instead, they give spontaneously, maybe based on an emotionally charged commercial they see on TV or need they hear about in church or at a fundraiser someone at work invites them to. They give spontaneously, as a reaction, but don't decide ahead of time how much and so when they give, they feel generous. But from God's perspective, they are not.

Many people want to be generous but can't, because they do their finances backwards. They buy first, pay bills second, and give last. In other words, when the paycheck comes, they go out to eat and go shopping, because their account is full. Then a few days later, they sit down and pay bills, and often realize they overspent. After that, if there's anything left over (often not), they give. But the gift is meager because it's leftovers.

I've learned that by giving first, paying second, and buying last, I've always had enough, and I'm able to find joy in being generous the way I want to be. It's because my giving is a priority and based on a percentage I decided on ahead of time.

If we are going to be New Testament kind of generous givers, then what we give must become a priority. We have to predetermine the percentage, and then give that off the top when we get paid.

Percentage

The second P is that, *percentage.* Remember, both the Old and New Testaments talk about giving by percentage.

What percentage should that be? Ultimately, it's between you and God. You read your Bible, you pray, and then you decide, believing what God would have you do in your budget. But predetermine a percentage and give that.

Should it be a tithe? Well, we are not under the law.

Personally, my wife and I have always tithed. Well, we started at 10%, but have increased over the years. In our way of thinking, if the Old Testament Jews were not nearly as wealthy as we are, and they were expected to tithe, we can too. In the New Testament, we are called to percentage based generous giving. It seems that less than a tithe for us would not be very generous. We started tithing when we were first married and could barely afford to put gas in our car or enough food on our table. But we figured out a way to tithe. And it has become a great blessing.

Here's a saying that has helped me:

> **The tithe as law has gone away;**
> **The tithe as principle is here to stay.**

If you have never tithed, the idea may seem so out there, so impossible for you, that you could not imagine doing it. I understand. So, pray about it, and between you and God, you decide what percentage of your income you should give. Then make that giving a priority. Give it off the top.

Progressive

The third principle is *progressive.* As our income increases, the percentage we give should also increase. This also comes from Paul's words in 1 Timothy 6:17-19.

You would think that rich people give more than poor people, wouldn't you? And most rich people think they give more than poor people, or middle-class people. But that's only because they see the dollar amounts of what they give. But remember Jesus' words to his disciples about the widow who gave the two small coins? She gave more than the rich who gave large amounts. Because God cares about percentages, not dollar amounts. So, the percentage we give ought to increase as our income increases.

In reality, as people's income increases, the percentage they give decreases, while their lifestyle increases even more. God says it should be the other way around. As our income increases, our giving percentage should also increase.

Yes, it's ok for our lifestyle to also improve. After all, Paul did say that in the 1 Timothy 6 passage that God gives us all things to enjoy. He's happy for our lifestyle to improve. But more than that, he wants to see our giving improve. And that only happens if the percentage we give increases.

So, God wants you to be a 3P giver: *priority*, *percentage*, *progressive*.

I'm not going to close this chapter with questions for you to write answers to. I just want you to spend some time, after studying the verses that are in this chapter, to pray and consider what the Lord would have you do. You don't need to write anything down, but consider these questions in your time as you pray, and then do something about the answers that come.

What time will I give to God for prayer and Bible reading? For corporate worship?

What ministry should I volunteer to serve in, where I can use my gifts, passions and experiences?

What percentage does he want me to start giving?

CHAPTER 12

Pass It On

S top and think for a moment. There have been people in your life who have made a great spiritual impact on you. It might be that their example caused you to pay attention to what they believed. It could be that they had the courage to start a conversation with you about God, which eventually led to you becoming a follower of Jesus. It could be the person doing this study with you.

Who has had the greatest spiritual influence on you?

Probably more than one person, but if you think about it, you can identify at least one or two individuals who took interest in you and helped you with major progress on your spiritual journey.

These same people had someone in their lives who did the same for them... on and on it could be traced all the way back to the earliest followers of Jesus. Because when Jesus called his disciples to become fishers of men, he taught them how to pass that privilege and responsibility on to those they would affect. You have been blessed by having others investing themselves in you and now God wants you to be that same blessing to others by investing yourself in them.

We're in the last chapter and coming to the end of this book. But hopefully, it's not the end for you. Because just as God has used people to help you grow, he now wants to use you to do the same for others.

Read 2 Timothy 2:2. This was written to Timothy. Who taught Timothy?

If you know the story of Paul's conversion, you know that Paul also had a mentor. His name was Barnabas. Now, what does Paul tell Timothy to do with what Paul taught him?

You might think you are not ready to lead someone else through this study. And that's good. You probably aren't. None of us ever are. That's actually a great way to think. By maintaining that humility, you'll be more dependent on the Holy Spirit to help you. You will also be more inviting to learn from. No one wants to be mentored by a know-it-all. Passing on what you have learned does not mean that you are going to teach another person everything they will need or want to know. You are not responsible for "filling their cup" so to speak. You are responsible to "empty your cup" into theirs. If you do your best to pass on what you have learned, God will fill in the blanks and bring along the right people to teach them further.

This is something you can do! Don't tune out now! You've come so far. Let's finish this project and learn how to pass on what you've learned to others.

That's one of the benefits of the way this book is designed. You can now, in turn, guide someone else through this book, as you have just gone through it. And by rereading the book along with another person who is seeking to know God or to grow, and going through the questions and discussing the reading with them, you will wind up learning even more than you did going through it the first time.

Identify candidates

This might be the hardest part of passing it on…finding the right person to meet with to go through the book. You certainly don't want to go around asking people, "Can I mentor you?" That would be weird, and people will run! But there are plenty of people around you who would love to have someone take the time to help them understand Christianity and the Bible. Especially those who have not yet received Jesus.

So, who?

First of all, pray for God to lead you so someone who you can mentor. Then look for people in your life who have been asking questions about your faith or about your church, or anything religious. Inquisitive minds learn best. People you may work with or relatives who have noticed a new-found interest in your life, or changes in you, and have asked you what's happened, they are prime candidates. If you talk about church at work or among your friends and they are at all curious about why you care about spiritual things, again, they are prime candidates.

You also want to pay attention to people who seem to follow you. If you look around, there are some people who seem to want to be with you. They may ask you other questions, that may not be spiritually related. Or they seem to be interested in your life, for whatever reason. If they seem to follow you in any way, this is an opportunity for you.

People going through difficult times are also good candidates for a study like this. Most of us became serious about our faith during a difficult time (pivotal circumstance). It usually takes hardship for us to let go of ourselves and to understand our need for God. So, if you know someone at work or your neighborhood or you family who is struggling through a divorce, a death, or health issue (themselves or a loved one), they may be open to doing this study.

There are probably people attending your church who are either very new to the faith, or yet to believe, who would want to learn from this study.

If you talk to one of your pastors, they might even arrange your first conversation. That's what the church is supposed to be doing: making disciples. This study is just that, its discipleship.

Build a relationship

Someone said, "No one cares how much you know until they know how much you care!" It may take months or a year, even years, to foster the kind of relationship with someone for them to know that you care about them and trust you to do a study like this. Not that you should wait years to ask, you should start right away building a relationship. In fact, I recommend that you identify a few candidates and start building relationships with each of them. As you pray for them, and ask God for direction, just the process of caring for them and getting interested in their world will lead to the right time to ask if they are interested in doing the study.

Ask about their family with sincere interest and check back later based on what they share. If they talk about one of their kids or another relative, follow-up at a later date asking how it's going with that relative. This sends the message that you care, and as a follower of Jesus, you should.

Invite them to your home for special events. Whenever you host a family gathering or a cookout with church friends, invite them. Include them in your world and your life.

When you are conversing with them, be interested in them. Always steer the conversation to them and their interests. Selfish people love to talk about themselves. Don't be that person. People don't enjoy hanging around with someone who goes on and on about themselves and their own interests. But they love being around people who care about them, and care enough to get interested in their lives and the things they enjoy. So, talk about them and what they want to talk about.

Additionally, always be transparent. Don't be that "church person" who pretends that everything is perfect, never having any apparent struggles. Let them see that you are like them, that you are flawed, but are grateful for God's forgiveness. Be real!

The key here is for you to be genuine. This is not a strategy for manipulating a relationship into a spiritual "notch on your belt." This is about doing what Jesus taught: genuinely caring about people and showing it by your words and actions. When you do, they will get interested in the God who is motivating you.

Offer to do a Bible study

Once the relationship has been established and trust has been earned, pray for and look for an opportunity to take the plunge and just ask them if they'd be interested in doing a Bible study with you. If this person has been asking you questions about God, your faith, or church, you can say something like, "You have a lot of good questions. I have a Bible study that teaches the basics of who God is, Christianity, and what the Bible is about. Would you be interested in doing it with me?"

If they express any interest, establish a time and place for your first get-together. I've done most of my mentoring in restaurants, though I've done it in their home and my home, depending on the comfort level of the person. Sometimes, a public place over breakfast, coffee, or lunch, works well. But sometimes they prefer the privacy of a home. Some have also done this study with a coworker before or after work. I've known people who did this in their car in the job place parking lot.

I've often said something like, "How about if we meet for coffee on Thursday mornings before work. I have a simple Bible study that gives a great introduction to what the Bible teaches."

The important thing is for you to have the courage to ask. We miss a lot of opportunities because we lack the courage to ask. Remember, you are not in this alone. You have the Holy Spirit preparing the person and speaking on the inside while you are making the ask on the outside.

They might say, "No." But that's ok. They also might say, "Sure." You'll never know if you don't ask.

If you get a "no," don't give up. The Lord has a way of working behind the scenes. I've done this same study with people who initially didn't want to, and later did the study with me, and then did it with others. If you are cultivating several relationships at the same time with this in mind, when you get a "no" from one, you can simply ask the next.

But it's important to have the courage to ask.

Go through this book with them

Before your first meeting, give them a copy of this book and tell them to read the introduction and the first chapter, and tell them that it'll be important for them to fill out the questions in the book as they are reading through it, because you will go through those questions with them when you get together. You may also want to give them a copy of a *New Living Translation* or *New International Version* of the Bible, so that they have an easy to understand copy of the Bible to use for the questions.

I know you've already read the book. After all, you're now on the last couple of pages. Congratulations! But it's important that they know you are reading the material along with them, as well as looking up and re-familiarizing yourself with the Scriptures that are in the book. And you will want to be prepared for your meeting. So, make sure that you read the material and look over the questions before the meeting. Mentally prepare yourself for how they might answer the questions and what other questions they might have for you. You might even highlight and make notes in the book that you may want to bring up and talk about in your meeting together.

A day or two before your first meeting, send them a text or an email, asking them how they are doing on the reading. It will be best for them to have read it and filled out the questions taking their time, rather than rushing through it right before you get together.

Start your meeting with prayer. Ask God to reveal himself to your friend and that both of you together will understand all that he wants you to know.

Then dig in to the questions in the book, and bring up those things that you have highlighted and made notes on. They will probably have some thoughts and questions themselves from their reading that they've made notes about in the book.

Take your time going through the book. Don't rush it. You will probably need to and should break some of the chapters. If you are able to cover a whole chapter, and they are understanding it, then doing one in a week is fine. But it's better to move slowly through the material, and break up the chapters by what you are able to cover, then to move too quickly through it.

This is very important: WATCH YOUR TIME. Respect the time they are giving to this and *don't let the meeting last more than an hour*. You might think things are going well and that they want it to go longer, but when a study lasts longer than an hour, they will only comprehend and digest so much. Limit yourself to an hour and strictly watch your time. It will help you and him as the study goes along. If you go longer than an hour, after a while, you'll start getting cancelations, rescheduling and even no-shows. But if they know they can trust you with the time, it will help their consistency.

Don't worry about questions you cannot answer. You are not going to know all the answers! Just admit it when you don't know and ask if you can get back to them. There are plenty of resources to go to in order to get answers. You can even respond via email after you look things up. That might help the study to do further dialog through the week by email. One of your pastors can also be a very helpful resource for you.

Get into their lives

Discipleship is not just a Bible Study. It's involving yourself in another person's life and walking with them to introduce them to Jesus, and then helping them to grow. So, get together for reasons other than the study. As I said earlier about building the relationship even before the study starts, don't stop after you start a Bible study. Stay interested and involved in their life and invite them to things with your friends/family and at church. Getting them around other Christians is an important step to helping people understand genuine Christianity. Church functions and events where there are other Christians is a big part of that. Get them around your spiritual family so they can see you are not the only one!

Pray

Pray for them weekly and let them know that you are. Pray that God opens their eyes to his grace and that the Holy Spirit will go far beyond what you are doing and draw them to him.

Also, pray with them in every meeting. A big part of teaching them what a relationship with God is like is by letting them hear you pray. I suggest you open and close each meeting with prayer.

Teach them to multiply

If they are doing this lesson with you, they'll get to this chapter just like you are now. And they'll smile because they'll realize that the Bible study you are doing together is in response to this chapter. That's great! In fact, a good way to encourage them to do the same is by sharing your own story of how you came to invite them into the study.

More than anything else, God wants to enjoy a relationship with us and then with those around us. He wants us to know him, to be forgiven for our sins and be reconciled with him, so that we can fulfill the purpose he created us for.

I'm so glad you were willing to read this and go through these questions, looking up all of the Scriptures. I know it's been a fair amount of work. But if the result is you knowing Christ, and making him known to others, then there is nothing else you could have put your time into that would have been more worthwhile!

ABOUT THE AUTHOR

Scott Ziegler has been a pastor for 30 years, and in ministry for 35 years. He was the Founding Pastor of Hillcrest Bible Church in Oregon, Wisconsin, where he ministered for 20 years. Today, he is the Lead Pastor of The Bridge Community Church, where he has served for 10 years. The Bridge (thebridge.church) is a vibrant and growing multi-campus church in Chicago's northwest suburbs.

Scott's heart for ministry has always focused primarily on sharing the Christian message with those who have been either turned off by religion, or have very little knowledge of God and the Bible. He is passionate about seeing lives transformed by the teaching of God's Word. Visit his blog at pastorscottz.com.

Scott and his wife, Linda, live in Des Plaines, Illinois and have 3 grown children and 3 grandchildren.

Made in the USA
Lexington, KY
31 December 2017